Englisch lernen – Bild für Bild

sprachen
ht

Wenn Sie das Buch durchgearbeitet haben, werden Sie die untenstehenden Sätze mühelos übersetzen können.

Eve saw the apple.

She took it.

She gave it to Adam.
Eve did these things.

The apple was seen by her.
It was taken by her.
It was given by her to Adam.
These things were done by Eve.

Englisch lernen – Bild für Bild

Von I. A. Richards und
Christine M. Gibson

Humboldt-Taschenbuchverlag

humboldt-taschenbuch 296
Umschlaggraphik: Christa Manner

Taschenbuchbearbeitung durch die Redaktion: Einführung in die Aussprache, phonetische Erklärungen im Text, deutsche Übersetzung der Wörterliste.

Druck: Presse-Druck Augsburg
Printed in Germany
ISBN 3–581–66296–5

Vorwort

Dieses Buch ist für den Anfänger gedacht, der die englische Sprache anhand von Bildern erlernen soll. Jede Seite ist nach dem Schema

1	2
3	4

zu lesen. In zusammenhängenden Sätzen, die sich unmittelbar auf die Bilder beziehen, werden etwa 500 der gebräuchlichsten englischen Wörter behandelt. Jede nachfolgende Lerneinheit baut auf der vorangegangenen auf. Dabei ist nach streng methodischen Gesichtspunkten vorgegangen worden.

Wenn man Seite um Seite den Bezug zwischen Bild und Text herstellt, lernt man die Anfangsgründe des Englischen spielend und ohne übermäßigen Gedächtnisaufwand. Übersetzungen in die Muttersprache sind auf jeden Fall zu vermeiden. Es sollten jeweils zwei bis drei Seiten solange geübt werden, bis der Lernende in der Lage ist, die zu den Bildern passenden Sätze ohne Hilfe englisch formulieren zu können. Er sollte von vornherein versuchen, die Texte nicht einfach auswendig zu lernen, sondern sie auch zu verstehen, kurz gesagt, englisch zu denken. Die Fragen, die in Abständen von ungefähr 30 Seiten im Text vorkommen, dienen der zusätzlichen Überprüfung der Kenntnisse. Sie sind auf englisch zu beantworten.

Taucht eine Vokabel zum ersten Mal im Text auf, so wird sie am unteren Rand der betreffenden Seite noch einmal zusammen mit der Lautschrift in eckigen Klammern aufgeführt. Die Aussprache wird durch die Symbole der International Phonetic Association wiedergegeben.

Ein Wörterverzeichnis am Ende des Buches bringt die Vokabeln des Hauptteils mit den entsprechenden Übersetzungen.

Die phonetischen Zeichen der International Phonetic Association

A. Vokale und Diphthonge

[ɑː]	wie in Vater	father [ˈfɑːðə*]
[ʌ]	kurzes dunkles a	butter [ˈbʌtə*]; come [kʌm]
[æ]	heller, ziemlich offener, nicht zu kurzer Laut	fat [fæt]; man [mæn]
[ɛə]	nicht zu offenes halblanges ä	bare [bɛə*]; pair [pɛə*]
[au]	helles zwischen ɑː und æ liegendes a und schwächeres u	house [haus]; now [nau]
[ei]	halboffenes e, nach i auslautend und i	make [meik]; they [ðei]; rain [rein]
[e]	etwas geschlossener als das e in Bett	bed [bed]; less [les]
[ə]	etwas geschlossener als das e in Gelage	about [əˈbaut]; butter [ˈbʌtə*]; nation [ˈneiʃən]; connect [kəˈnekt]
[*ə*]	schwächeres [ə]	question [ˈkwestʃ*ə*n]
[iː]	etwas offener einsetzend als in lieb, Bibel	me [miː]; sheep [ʃiːp]; clean [kliːn]; chief [tʃiːf]
[i]	wie in bin, mit	it [it]; money [ˈmʌni]; give [giv]
[iə]	halboffenes halblanges i mit nachhallendem ə	ear [iə*]; idea [aiˈdiə]; here [hiə*]
[ou]	halboffenes langes o, in schwaches u auslautend	note [nout]; coat [kout]; know [nou]; go [gou]
[ɔː]	offener langer, zwischen ɑ und o schwebender Laut	door [dɔː*]; ball [bɔːl]; four [fɔː*]
[ɔ]	offener kurzer, zwischen ɑ und o schwebender Laut	shop [ʃɔp]; what [wɔt]; song [sɔŋ]
[əː]	offenes langes ö, kein Vorstülpen oder Runden der Lippen	word [wəːd]; girl [gəːl]; learner [ˈləːnə*]

[ɔi]	offenes o, die Zunge hebt sich halbwegs zur i-Stellung, schwächeres offenes i	voice [vɔis]; boy [bɔi]
[uː]	langes u wie in **Bu**ch, jedoch ohne Lippenrundung	shoe [ʃuː]; blue [bluː]; too [tuː]
[uə]	halboffenes halblanges u mit nachhallendem ə	our [′auə*]; hour [′auə*]
[u]	sehr kurzes u	full [ful]; book [buk]

B. Konsonanten

[r]	Nur vor Vokalen gesprochen. Völlig verschieden vom deutschen r. Die Zungenspitze bildet mit der oberen Zahnwulst eine Enge, durch die der Ausatmungsstrom mit Stimmton hindurchgetrieben wird, ohne den Laut zu rollen. Am Ende eines Wortes wird r nur bei Bindung mit dem Anlautvokal des folgenden Wortes gesprochen.	rail [reil]; red [red]; there is [ðɛər′iz]
[ʒ]	wie in **G**enie, **J**ournal	pleasure [′pleʒə*]; measure [′meʒə*]
[ʃ]	wie in **Sch**nee, ra**sch**	crushing [′krʌʃiŋ]; sugar [′ʃugə*]; addition [ə′diʃən]
[θ]	stimmloser Lispellaut. Durch Anlegen der Zunge an die oberen Schneidezähne hervorgebracht	thin [θin]
[ð]	derselbe Laut wie θ, nur stimmhaft	there [ðɛə*]; then [ðen]; father [′fɑːðə*]
[s]	wie in Spa**ß**, rei**ß**en	see [siː]
[z]	stimmhaftes s wie in sausen	leaves [liːvz]; boys [bɔiz]
[ŋ]	wie in fa**ng**en, si**ng**en	doing [′duiŋ]

[ŋk]	wie in senken, Wink	bank [bæŋk]
[w]	flüchtiges, mit Lippe an Lippe gesprochenes w, aus der Mundstellung für uː gebildet	well [wel]; one [wʌn]; which [witʃ]
[f]	wie in flott, Pfeife	fat [fæt]
[v]	wie in Vase, Ventil	very [ˈveri]
[j]	flüchtiger, zwischen j und i schwebender Laut	yes [jes]; young [jʌŋ]

— Die Betonung der englischen Wörter wird durch das Zeichen [ˈ] vor der zu betonenden Silbe wiedergegeben.

— Das Zeichen [*] gibt an, daß das r am Ende eines Wortes nur bei Bindung mit dem Anlautvokal eines folgenden Wortes gesprochen wird.

— Die Länge eines Vokals wird durch [ː] bezeichnet, z. B. arm [ɑːm].

I

YOU

I

YOU

I [ai]

you [ju:]

HE

SHE

IT

THEY

he [hi:]
she [ʃi:]

it [it]
they [ðei]

HE

THEY

IT

THEY

I am here.

He is there.

She is here.

She is there.

am [æm]
is [iz]

here [hiə*]
there [ðɛə*]

It is here.

It is there.

They are here.

They are there.

are [ɑ:*]

You are there.

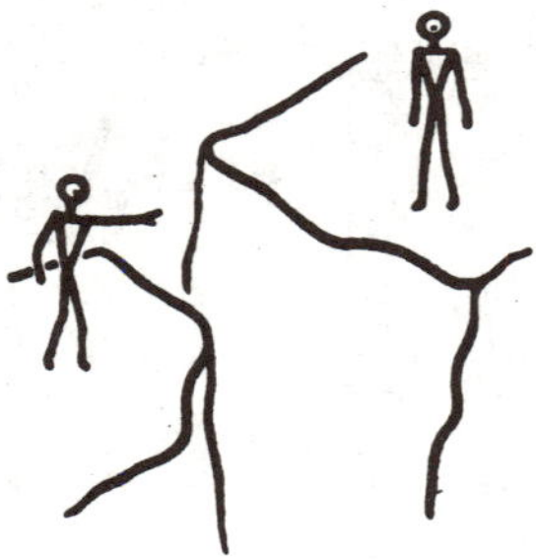

You are there.

You are here.

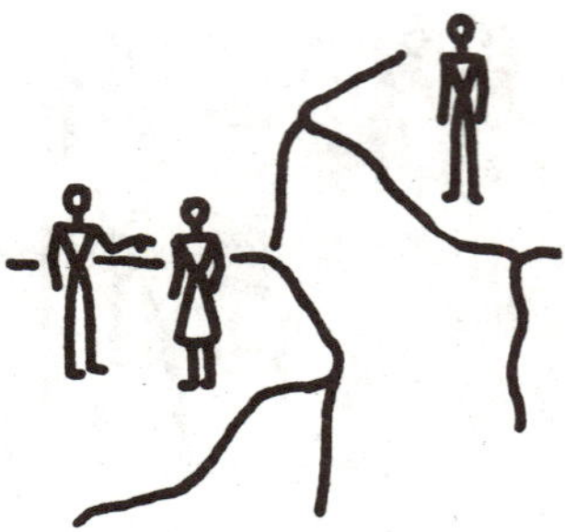

We are here.

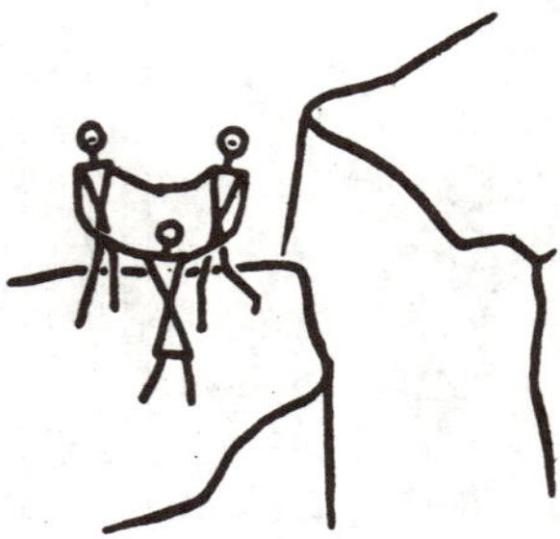

we [wi:]

It is there.

They are there.

We are here.

They are here.

This is a man.

This is a woman.

That is a man.

That is a woman.

this [ðis]
a [ə]
man [mæn]

woman [ˈwumən]
that [ðæt]

This man is here.

That man is there.

This woman is here.

That woman is there.

This is a table.
This table is here.

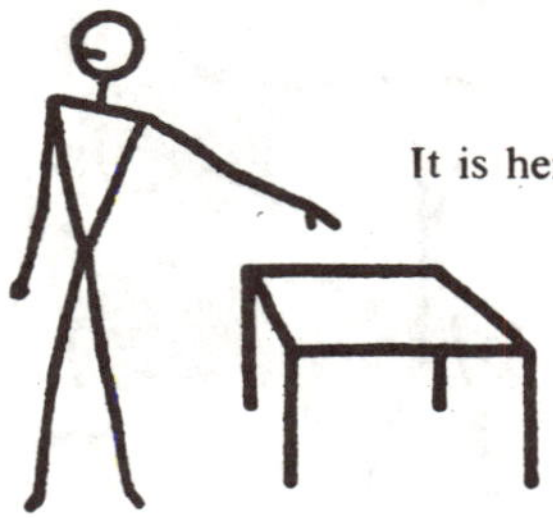

That is a table.
That table is there.

This is a hat.
It is a hat.

This is a hand.

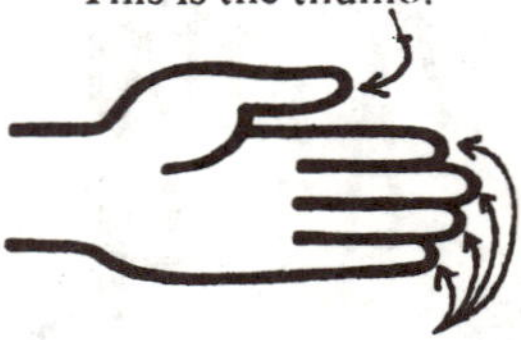

table [ˈteibl]
hat [hæt]
hand [hænd]
the [ðə]

thumb [θʌm]
these [ði:z]
fingers [ˈfiŋgəz]

This is my head.

This is my hat.

My hat is in my hand.
It is in my hand.

My hat is on my head.
It is on my head.

my [mai]
head [hed]

in [in]
on [ɔn]

This is my hat.

That is his hat.

His hat is on his head.

Her hat is in her hand.

his [hiz]

her [hə:*]

That is your hat.
It is on the table.

Those are your hats.
They are on the table.

These are my hands.

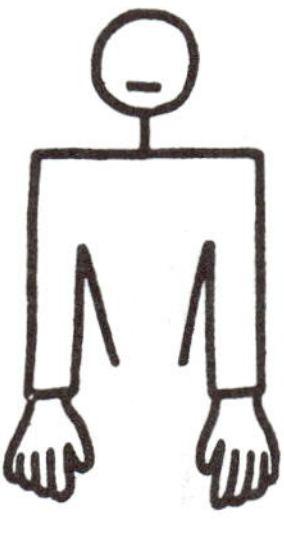

This is
my
right
hand.

This is
my
left
hand.

Those are your hands.

That is
your
right
hand.

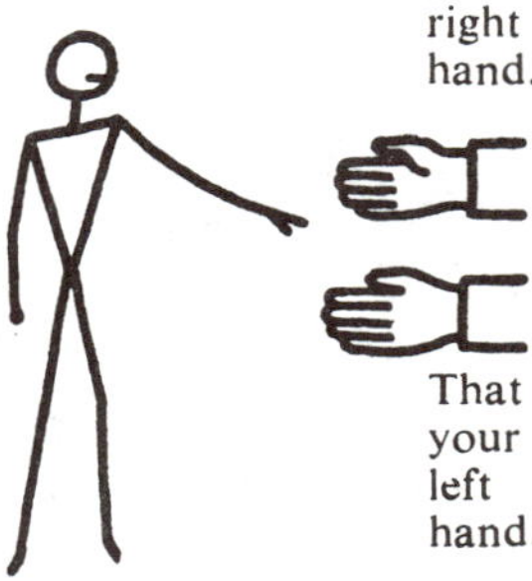

That is
your
left
hand.

your [jɔ:*]
those [ðouz]

right [rait]
left [left]

His hat is on the table.

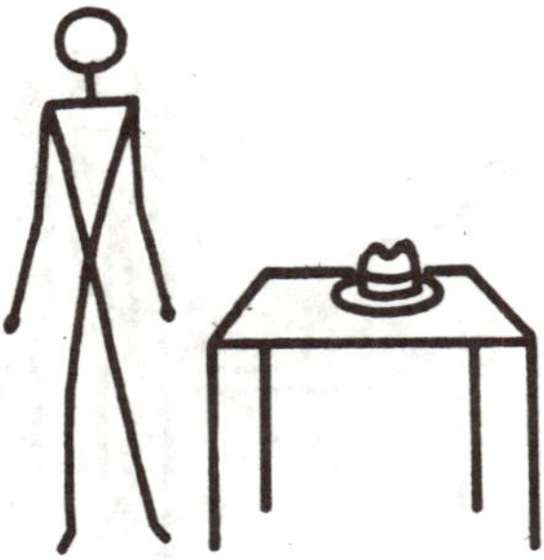

He will take his hat off the table.

He is taking it off the table.

He took it off the table.

will take [wəl'teik]
off [ɔ:f]

is taking [iz'teikiŋ]
took [tuk]

He will put his hat on his head.

He is putting his hat on his head.

He put his hat on his head.
He put it on.

It was on the table.
It is on his head.

will put [wəl'put]
is putting [iz'putiŋ]

put [put]
was [wɔz]

He will take his hat off his head.

He is taking his hat off his head.

His hat is in his hand.
It was on his head.

He took his hat off.

It is in his hand.

This is a hat.

These are hats.

This is a hand.

These are hands.

This is a man.

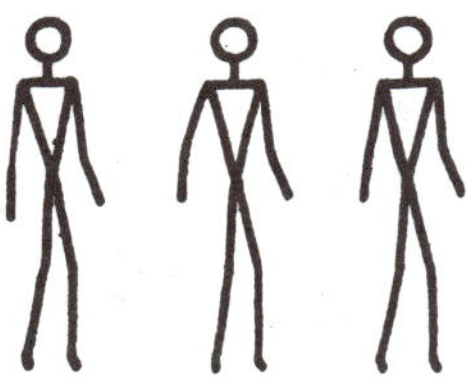

These are men.

This is a table.

These are tables.

This is a woman.

These are women.

hats [hæts]
hands [hænds]
tables [teiblz]

men [men]
women [ˈwimin]

This is a man.

This is
his hand.

It is the man's hand.

This is a man's hat.
It is on a man's head.

Now it is in the man's hands.
It is in his hands.

This is a woman.

This is
her hand.

It is the woman's hand.

This is a woman's hat.
It is on a woman's head.

Now it is in the woman's hands.
It is in her hands.

now [nau]

He will give his hat to the man.

He is giving his hat to the man.

He gave it to the man.
He gave it to him.

It is in the man's hands now.

will give [wəl'giv]
to [tu]
is giving [iz'giviŋ]

gave [geiv]
him [him]

The man will give his hat to the woman.

He is giving his hat to the woman.

He gave it to the woman.
He gave it to her.

It is in the woman's hands now.

The woman will put the hat on the table.

She is putting it on the table.

She put it there.

It was in her hand.
It is on the table.

This is a ship.

These are ships.

This ship is in the bottle.

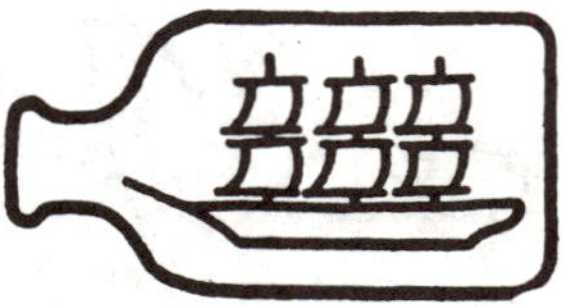

These ships are on the water.

This is water.

ship [ʃip]
bottle [ˈbɔtl]

water [ˈwɔːtə*]

This is water.

This is a bottle.

The bottle
is in a
man's hand.

This is a glass.
It is on the table.

Now the glass is off the table.

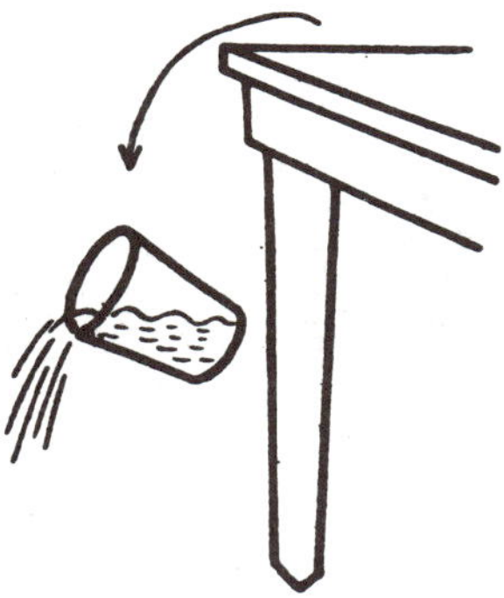

The glass and the water are on the floor.

glass [glɑ:s]
floor [flɔ:*]

and [ənd]

This is a bottle

and this
is a bottle.

This
and
this are bottles.

This is a glass

and this is
a glass.

These are glasses.

That is a bird and
that is a bird.
Those are birds.
They are birds.

That man and that
woman are there.

This man and this
woman are here.

bottles [ˈbɔtlz]
glasses [ˈglɑ:siz]

bird [bə:d]

This is a man.

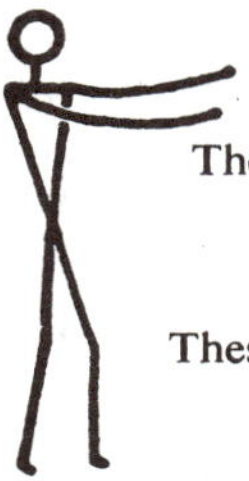

These are his arms.

These are his legs.

These are his feet.

This is an arm.

This is a leg.

This is a foot.

This is a table.

These are its legs.

Its feet are on the floor.

This is a chair.

These are its arms.

These are its legs.

Its feet are on the floor.

arms [ɑ:mz]
legs [legz]
feet [fi:t]
an [ən]
arm [ɑ:m]

leg [leg]
foot [fut]
its [its]
chair [tʃɛə*]

This is a room.

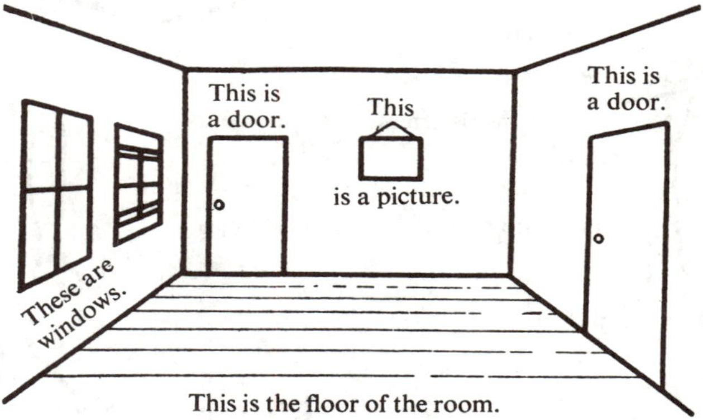

These are the windows of the room.

This is a window and this is a window.

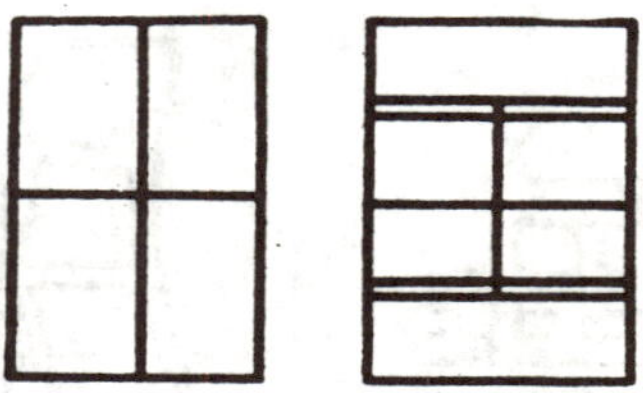

room [ru:m]
door [dɔ:*]
picture [ˈpiktʃə*]
windows [ˈwindouz]

of [ɔv; əv]
shut [ʃʌt]
open [ˈoupən]

This door is open.

This door is shut.

This is a wall of the room.

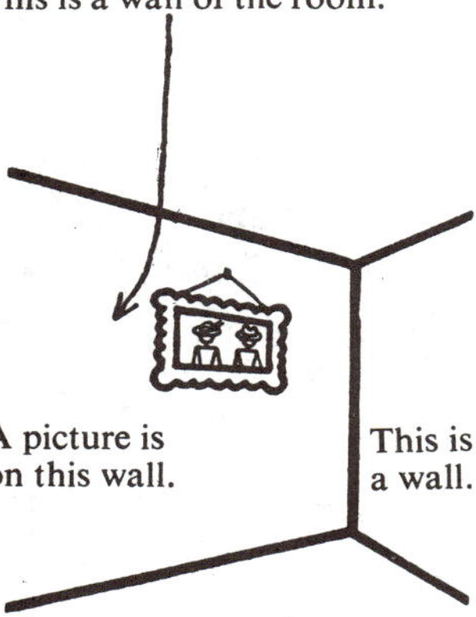

This is the floor of the room.

This is a picture of a man and a woman.

This is the cord of the picture.

This is a hook.

This is the frame of the picture.

wall [wɔ:l]
cord [kɔ:d]

hook [huk]
frame [freim]

This is a house.

These are houses.

house [haus]
houses [ˈhauziz]

street [stri:t]

The man
will go
to his house.

He
is going
to his house.

The man went
to his house.
He is there.

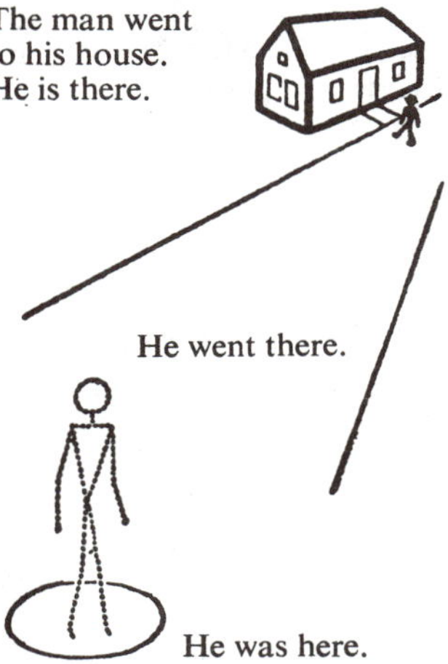

He is at his door.

He is at the door of his house.

will go [wəlˈgou]
is going [izˈgo*u*iŋ]

went [went]
at [æt; ət]

What is this?
It is a hat.
"What is this?" is a question.
"It is a hat," is an answer.

This is a question mark.

We put question marks after questions.

"Is this a hat?"
That is a question.
"Yes, it is."
That is an answer.

"Is this a hat?"
"No, it is *not* a hat. It is a hand."
That is an answer.

what [wɔt]
question [ˈkwestʃən]
answer [ˈɑ:nsə*]
question mark [ˈkwestʃənmɑ:k]

after [ˈɑ:ftə*]
yes [jes]
no [nou]
not [nɔt]

QUESTIONS

a What is this?
It is a

b What is this?

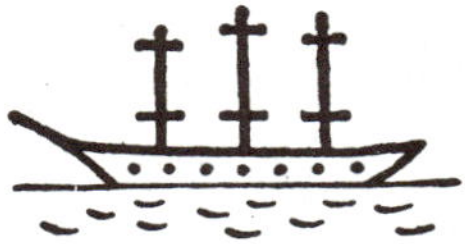

c What is this?

d What is this?

e What is this?

f What is this?

g What is this?

h What is this?

This page is page 31. The answers are on page 34.

questions [ˈkwestʃənz]
page [peidʒ]
answers [ˈɑ:nsəz]

31 [ˈθə:tiˈwʌn]
34 [ˈθə:tiˈfɔ:*]

a What are these?

And what is this?

b What are these?

And what is this?

c What are these?

And what is this?

d What are these?

And what is this?

e What are these?

And what is this?

f What is this?

And what is this?

g What are these?

And what is this?

h What is this?

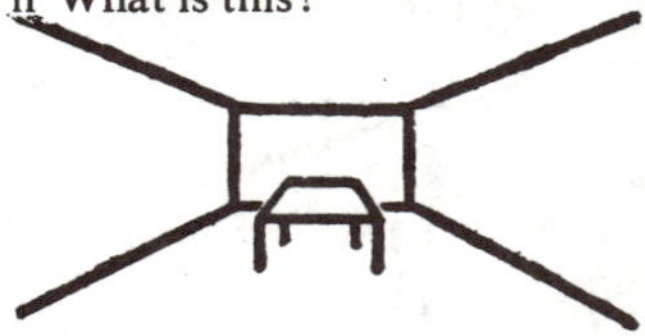

What is in it?

This page is page 32. The answers are on page 34.

32 ['θə:ti'tu:]

QUESTIONS

a Is the hat on the table?

b Is the man in the room?

c Is the picture on the wall?

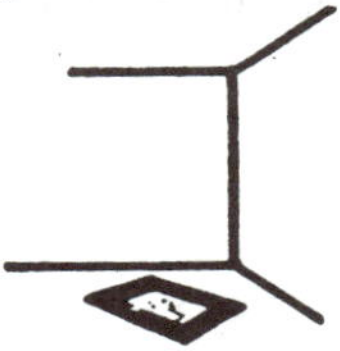

d Is the bird on the seat?

e Is the glass in the woman's hand?

f Is the water in the glass?

g Is this ship in a bottle?

h Are the man and the woman at the door?

This page is page 33. The answers are on page 34.

seat [si:t] 33 [ˈθə:tiˈθri:]

These are answers to questions on pages 31, 32 and 33. This page is page 34.

Page 31

a It is a house.
b It is a ship.
c It is a table.
d It is a bottle.
e It is a leg.
f It is an arm.
g It is a leg of a table.
h It is an arm of a chair.

Page 32

a They are three men. That is a woman.
b They are glasses.
That is a glass.
c They are fingers.
That is the thumb.
d They are windows.
That is a door.
e They are houses.
That is a street.
f It is a picture of a man and a house.
That is the frame of the picture.
(Its frame.)
g They are feet.
That is a foot.
h That is a room.
A table is in it.

Page 33

a Yes, it is.
b Yes, he is.
c No, it is not.
It is on the floor.
d No, it is not.
It is on the floor.
e No. It is in the man's hand.
f No, it is not in the glass.
g No. It is on the water.
h Yes, they are at the door.

pages [ˈpeidʒiz]

three [θriː]

What is this?
This is a clock.
What is the time?
The time is one (1:00).
One hand is at one.

What is the time?
The time is two (2:00).
It was one (1:00).
It will be three (3:00).

What is the time?
The time is four (4:00).
It was three (3:00).
It will be five (5:00).

What is the time?
Now the time is six (6:00).
Is was five (5:00).
It will be seven (7:00).

clock [klɔk]
time [taim]
one [wʌn]
will be [wəl'bi:]

four [fɔ:*]
five [faiv]
six [siks]
seven ['sevn]

What is the time?
Now the time is eight (8:00).
It was seven (7:00).
It will be nine (9:00).

What is the time?
Now the time is ten (10:00).
It was nine (9:00).
It will be eleven (11:00).

What is the time?
The time is twelve
(12:00).
It was eleven (11:00).
It will be one (1:00).
The two hands are at twelve now.

These are the numbers from one to twelve.
One, two, three, four, five, six, seven, eight, nine, ten, eleven, twelve.

eight [eit]
nine [nain]
ten [ten]
eleven [iˈlevn]

twelve [twelv]
numbers [ˈnʌmbəz]
from [frɔm]

What are things?

A house is a thing.
Houses are things.

A hat is a thing. Hats are things.

Doors and windows are things.
Tables and chairs are things.

This is a man.

This is a woman.

This is a boy.

This is a girl.

Men and women and boys and girls are not things.
They are persons.
You are a person.

There are two persons in this room.
They are a boy and a girl.

The girl is at the door.
The boy is at the window.

The girl will go to the window.

She will be with the boy at the window.
She will be with him at the window.

things [θiŋz]
a thing [ə 'θiŋ]
boy [bɔi]
girl [gə:l]

persons ['pə:snz]
a person [ə'pə:sn]
with [wið]

The girl is going to the window.
Where was she?

She was at the door.

She went to the window.
Where is she now?
She is at the window now.

She is with the boy.

They are at the window together.
She is with him at the window.
He is with her at the window.

These books are together on the shelf.

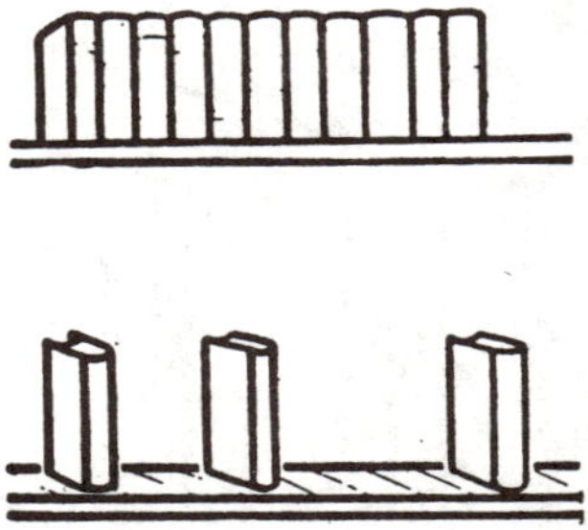

These books are not together.
They are on the shelf, but they are not together.

where [wɛə*]
together [tə'geðə*]
books [buks]

shelf [ʃelf]
but [bʌt]

The girl and the boy will go from the window.

They are going from the window.
They were at the window.

They went from the window.
She went with him and he went with her.

Now they are at the door together.
The boy is with the girl at the door.
She is at the door again.

were [wə:*]
are going [a:ˈgouiŋ]

again [əˈgen]

This is my head.

That is her head.

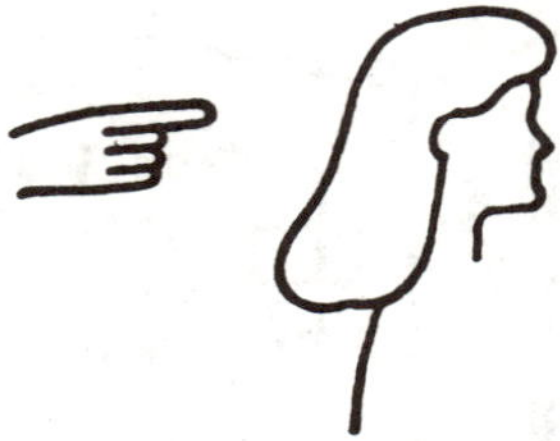

These are my eyes.

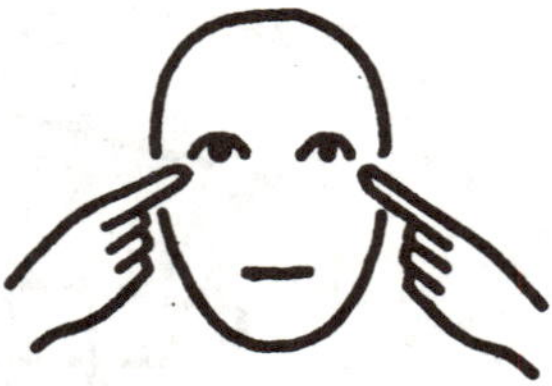

This is one eye.

This is the other eye.

Her eyes are open.

Her eyes are shut.

eyes [aiz]
eye [ai]

the other [ðiˈʌðə*]

My eyes are open.
I see.
Her eyes are shut.
She does not see.

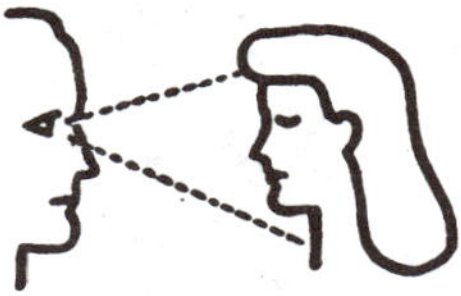

I see her.
She does not see me.

Now her eyes are open.
She sees.
What does she see?
She sees me.

I see her.
Our eyes are open.

Her eyes are open.

She sees.
They were shut.
She did not see.

She did not see me.

Her eyes are shut.

They were open.
She saw.
What did she see?

She saw me.

---

see [si:]
does [dʌz; dəz]
sees [si:z]
me [mi]

our [ˈauə*]
did [did]
saw [sɔ:]

A man has two eyes.
I have two eyes.

These are my eyes.

A man has a nose.
I have a nose.

This is my nose.

This man's mouth is open.
He is saying "mouth".

His mouth is shut.

He is not saying "mouth".

A man has a mouth.
I have a mouth.

This is my mouth.

His mouth is shut.
He will say "mouths".

He is saying "mouths".

He said "mouths".
He is not saying "mouths" now.
His mouth is shut again.

has [hæz]
have [hæv]
nose [nouz]
mouth [mauθ]

is saying [iz'seiiŋ]
will say [wəl'sei]
mouths [mauθz]
said [sed]

These are three books.

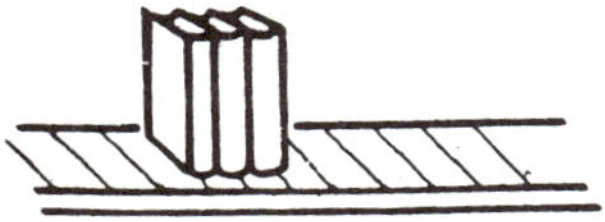

They are on a shelf.

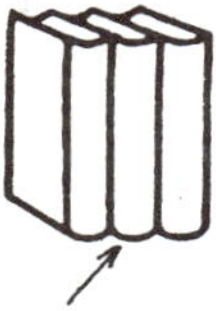

This book is between the other two books.

These are the pages of the book.

These are the covers of the book.

The pages are between the covers of the book.

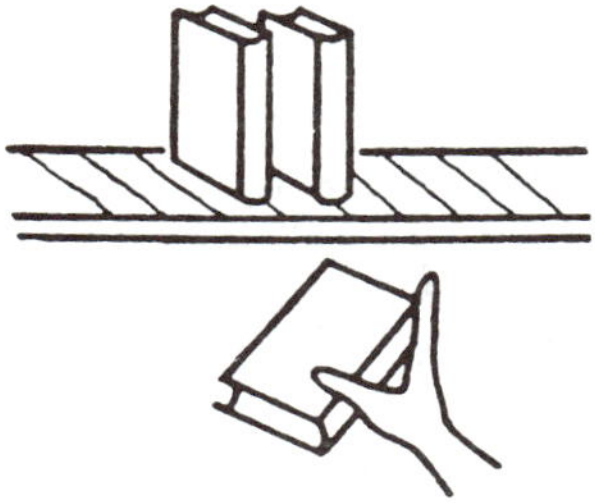

I have the book in my hand now. It was on the shelf. It was between the other two books on the shelf.

These are the fingers of my hand.

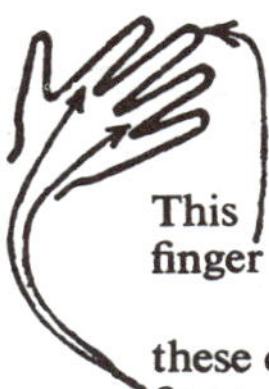

This finger is between these other two fingers of my hand.

between [bi'twi:n]

covers ['kʌvəz]

My nose is between my eyes.

And it is between my eyes and my mouth.

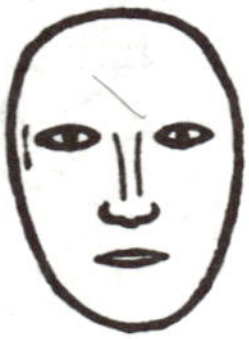

My mouth is under my nose.

My nose is over my mouth.
Our noses are over our mouths.

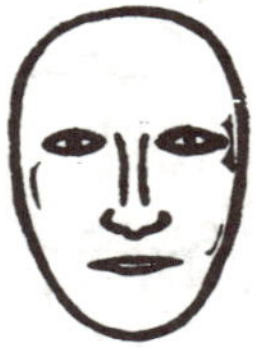

The light is over the table.

The dog is under the table.

This is a clock.

It is on the wall.
It is over the bookshelves.

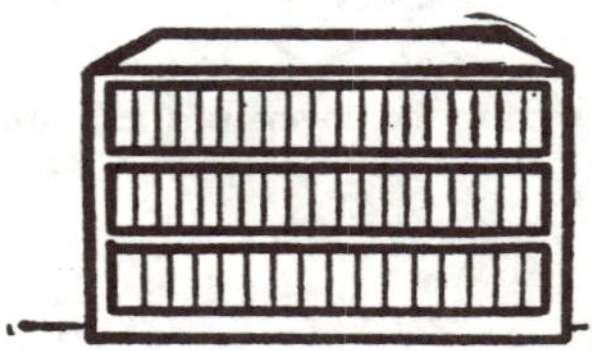

The bookshelves are under the clock.

under [ˈʌndə*]
over [ˈouvə*]
noses [nouziz]

light [lait]
dog [dɔg]
bookshelves [ˈbukʃelvz]

This is his hair.
It is short.

This is her hair.
It is long.

This is his head.

This is his face.
His eyes, his nose, and his mouth are parts of his face.

These are his ears.

Where are her ears?
They are under her hair.

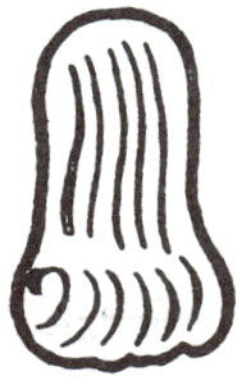

Her hair is over her ears.

This is a clock.

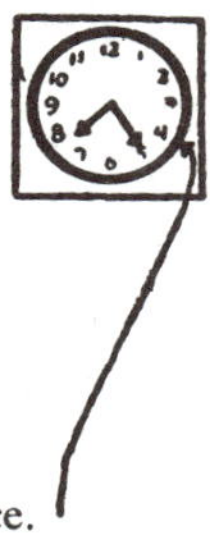

It has a face.
This is the face of the clock. The clock has two hands, a long hand and a short hand. The long hand is at 5. The short hand is between 7 and 8.

---

hair [hɛə*]
short [ʃɔ:t]
long [lɔŋ]

ears [iəz]
face [feis]
part [pɑ:t]

A clock has a face.

It has no nose.

It has no eyes.

It has no mouth.

It has no ears.

It has no hair but it has a face.

It has a face and two hands, the long hand

and the short hand.

The long hand of the clock is between one and two.
One is before two. Two is between one and three. Three is after two and two is after one.

I have this book in my hands.
It was on the shelf with the other books.
It was between the other two books before
I took it from the shelf.

before [biˈfɔ:*]

I have it in my hand.
I am putting it between the other two books.
Then it will be with the other books.

Now it is on the shelf again. It was in my hand. I had it in my hand. It is not in my hand.
Where is it?

This is a room.
What do you see in the room?
Do you see the floor and three walls of the room?
Do you see them?

Do you see a door and two windows?
Is one of the windows open?
Is the other window shut?
Do you see two chairs and the bookshelves between them?
Do you see the clock over the bookshelves?
Yes. I see them.
These things are in the room. The room is in a house.

then [ðen]
had [hæd]
do [də]

do you see [dju:ˈsi:]
them [ðem]

This is a face.

Eyes, nose, and mouth are parts of a face.

Which are the eyes?
Which is the nose?
Which is the mouth?

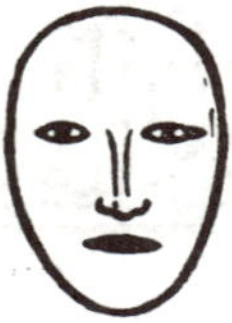

These are my hands.
Which is my right hand?
Which is my left hand?
Which are my thumbs?
Which are my fingers?

This is a man.
Which are his arms?
Which are his hands?
Which are his legs?
Which are his feet?

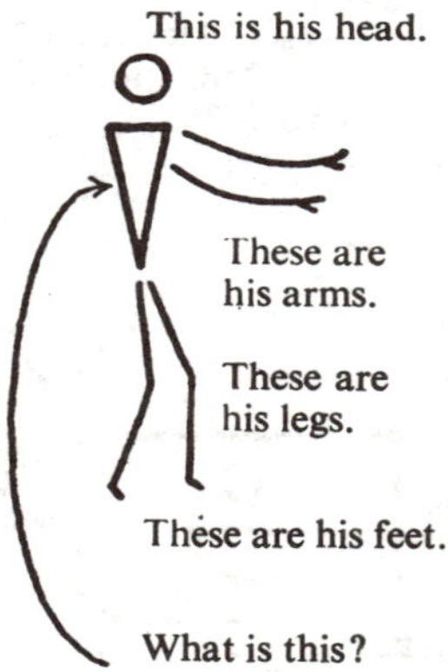

which [witʃ]

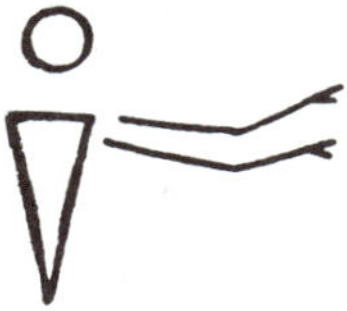

This is his body.

His head, his arms, his legs, and his body are parts of a man.

All men and
women and boys and girls have bodies.

This baby has a body.

This dog has a body.

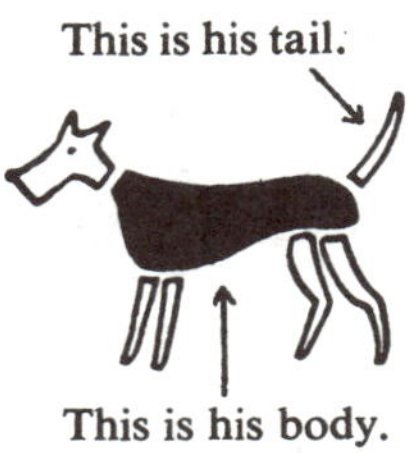

He has four legs and a head and a tail. He has no arms or hands, but he has feet. His head, his body, his legs, and his tail are parts of a dog.

This is a dog's head.

Which is his mouth?
Which are his eyes?
Which are his ears?
Which is his nose?

body [ˈbɔdi]
all [ɔːl]
bodies [ˈbɔdiz]

baby [ˈbeibi]
tail [teil]
or [ɔː*]

This is a foot.

These are toes.

They are parts of a foot.
These parts of a foot are its toes.

This is a toe. 

This is a leg.

This is a knee.
It is part of a leg.

This part of a leg is its knee.

Our legs are parts of us.

This is a neck.

It is a part of a man. It is between his head and his body.
The part which is between his head and his body is his neck.

This is a man's head.

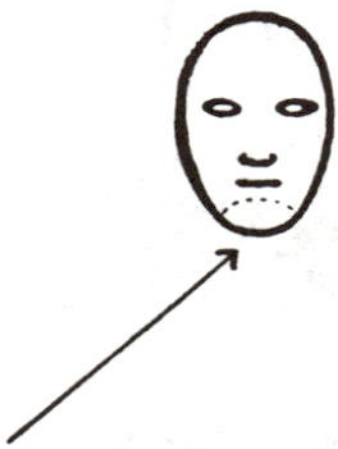

This is his chin.
It is under his mouth.
It is a part of his face.
The part which is under his mouth is his chin.

toes [touz]
toe [tou]
knee [ni:]

us [ʌs]
neck [nek]
chin [tʃin]

This is a man's body.

The part which is between his head, his arms, and his legs is his body.

This man has his finger on his chin.

This man has his hand on his chest.

This is his body.

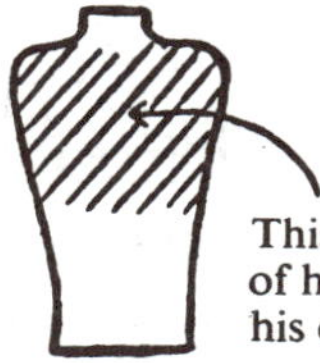

This part of him is his chest.

This is a chest of drawers.

This baby is on his hands and knees.

This baby is on his hands and feet.

This baby is on his knees.

This baby is on his feet.

chest [tʃest]
chest of drawers
[ˈtʃest əv ˈdrɔːəz]

knees [niːz]

QUESTIONS Where is the dog?

a

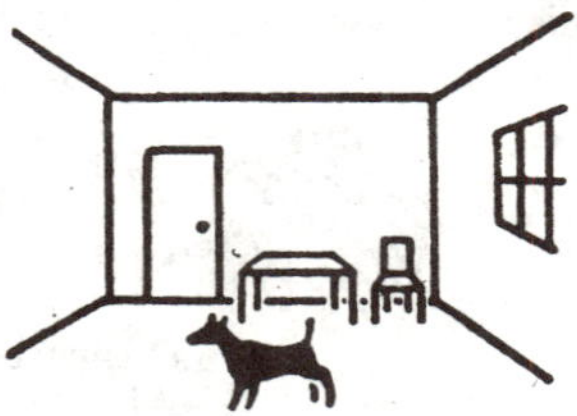

b

c

d

e

f

g

h

Answers to these questions are on page 56.

56 [ˈfiftiˈsiks]

QUESTIONS What do you see?

a

b

c

d

e

f

g

h

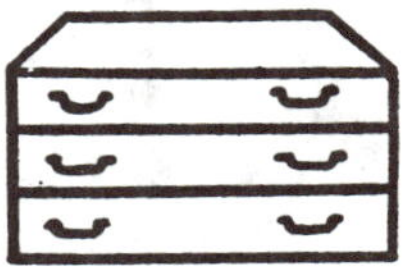

Answers to these questions are on page 56.

a

b

c

d

e

f

g

h

Answers to these questions are on page 57.

QUESTIONS What do you see?

a

b

c

d

Answers to these questions are on page 57.

Answers to questions on pages 52-53.

Page 52

a The dog is in a room.
b He is at the door.
c He is at the window.
d He is under the chair.
e He is under the table.
f He is on the table.
g He is between the table and the chair.
h He is on the chair.

Page 53

a I see a clock. The time is four.
b I see a man's face.
c I see a woman's face.
d I see a baby. He is on his hands and knees.
e I see two books. One of them is open. The other is shut.
f I see two girls. One of them is giving a book to the other.
g I see two babies. One of them is on his hands and knees. The other is on his feet.
h I see a chest of drawers.

52 [ˈfiftiˈtuː]
53 [ˈfiftiˈθriː]

babies [ˈbeibiz]

Answers to questions on pages 54-55.

Page 54

a He is saying, "These are my ears."

b He is saying, "This is my mouth."

c He is saying, "These are my eyes."

d He is saying, "This is my thumb."

e He is saying, "This finger is between these fingers."

f He is saying, "This is my nose."

g He is saying, "This is my hair."

h He is saying, "This is my head."

Page 55

a I see a boy and a girl. They are at a window.

b I see a clock on a table. The time is four.

c I see a room. It has two chairs in it. It has two windows and a door. One of the windows is open. The other window is shut. The door of the room is open. A picture is on the wall.

d I see a man. He has his finger on his chin. One of his eyes is open. The other eye is shut. His mouth is shut. He has no hair on his head.

54 [ˈfiftiˈfɔ:*]

55 [ˈfiftiˈfaiv]

Who is this?
He is John Smith.
His name is John Smith.
Where is John Smith?
He is at the door of his house.

He has his hand in his pocket.

He is taking a key from his pocket.

This is a key.

These are other keys.

who [hu:]
John [dʒɔn]
Smith [smiθ]
name [neim]

pocket [ˈpɔkit]
key [ki:]
keys [ki:z]

He will put the key in the lock of the door.

He is putting the key in the lock.

He is giving a turn to the key.

He is giving a push to the door. The door is open now.

lock [lɔk]
is giving a turn
[iz'giviŋ ə 'tə:n]

is giving a push
[iz'giviŋ ə 'puʃ]

John took the key from the lock.
He is putting it in his pocket.
He will go into his house.

He is going into the house.

He went into the house.
He is in the house.
The door is shut.

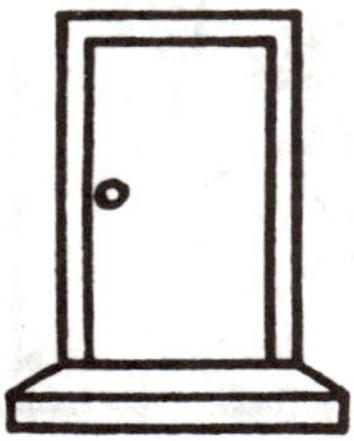

This is a room in the house.
Is John in the room?
No, he is not.

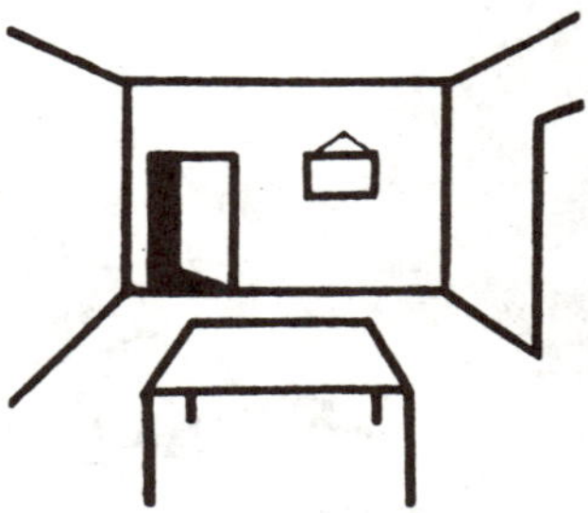

He will come into the room.

into [ˈintu]

will come [wəlˈkʌm]

He is coming into the room.
He will go to the table.

Mr. Smith came into the room.
He went to the table.

Is Mrs. Smith in the room?

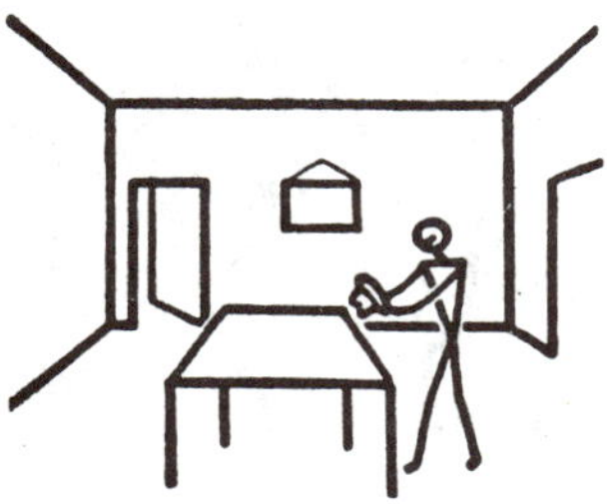

No, she is not.

She is in the house but she is not in the room.
She is in another room in the house.

Who is this?
This is Mary Smith. She is Mrs. Smith.
Her name is Mary Smith.

Mr [ˈmistə*]
came [keim]
Mrs [ˈmisiz]

another [əˈnʌðə*]
Mary [ˈmɛəri]

This is one of the doors of the room.

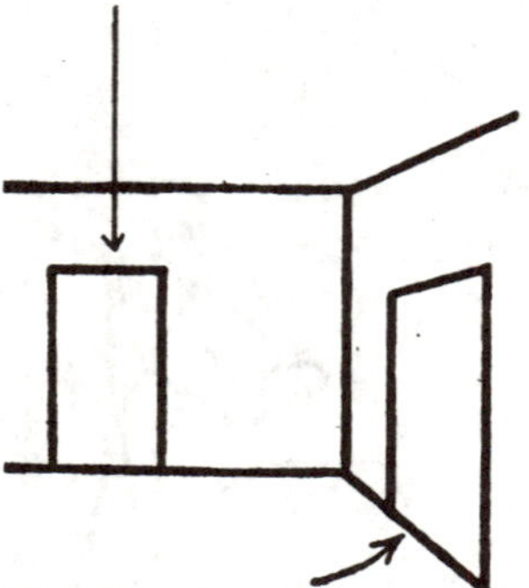

This is the other door.

This is one of the windows of the room.

One window is open.
The other windows are shut.

This is one of my hands.
It is my left hand.

This is my other hand.
It is my right hand.

This is one of my fingers.

This is my left thumb.

These are the other fingers of my left hand.

Mrs. Smith is not in the room.
She went out of the room.

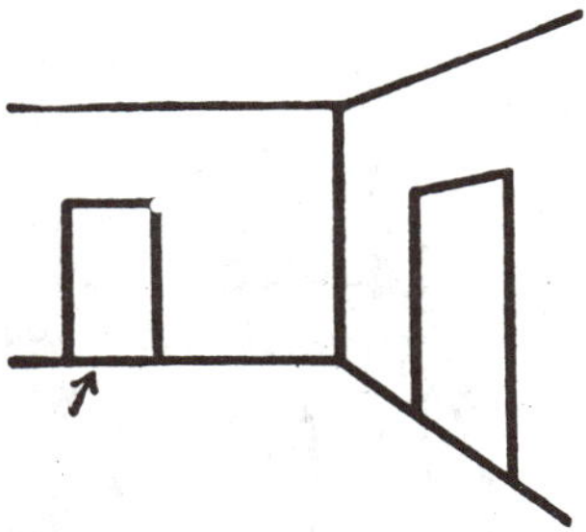

She went through this door.

Mr. Smith is in the room.
He came into the room.

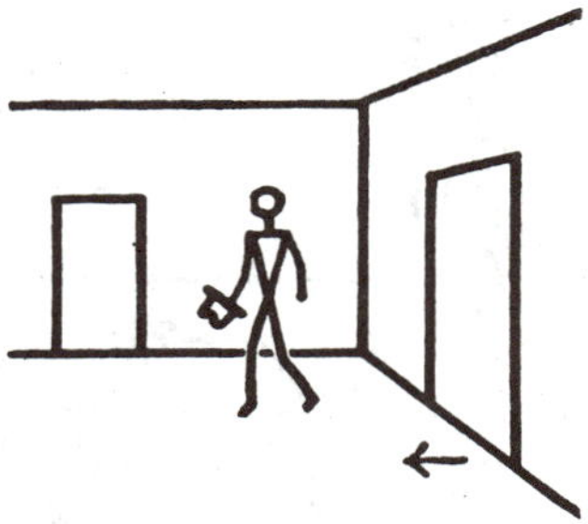

He came through this door.

Mr. Smith is putting his hat on the table.

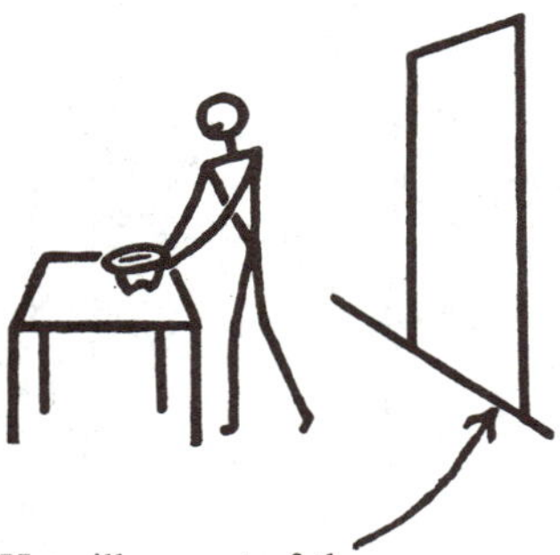

He will go out of the room through this door.

He put his hat on the table.
It is on the table now.

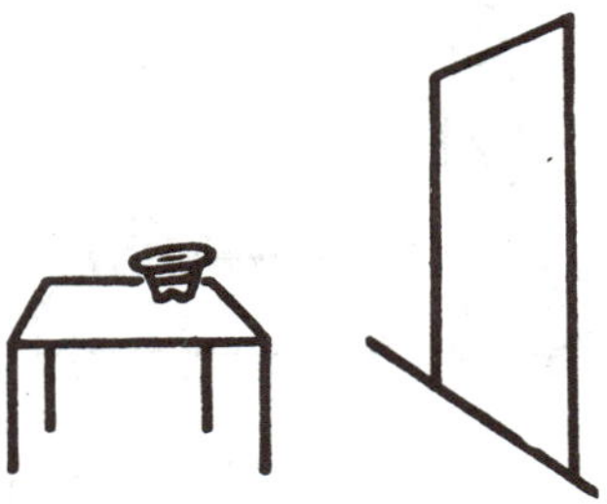

He went out of the room through this door.

out of [ˈautəv]

through [θru:]

Mary is coming into the room.

She is going to the table.

She will see the hat.

She sees it.

She saw it.
When did she see it?
She saw it after she went to the table.

when [wen]

She will take the hat in her hand.

She is taking it.

She took it in her hand.
She is going out of the room.

She has the hat in her hand.

She went out of the room with John's hat.

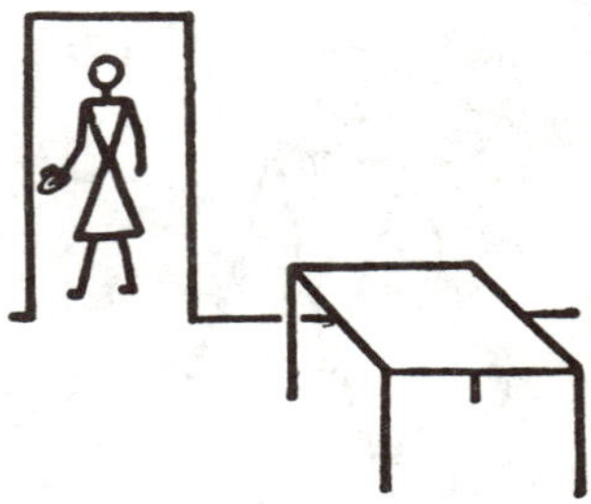

She is in another room now.
She came into this room through this door.

She has the hat with her.

What are these?
They are hooks.

That is another hat.
It is on a hook.

She will put John's hat on a hook.

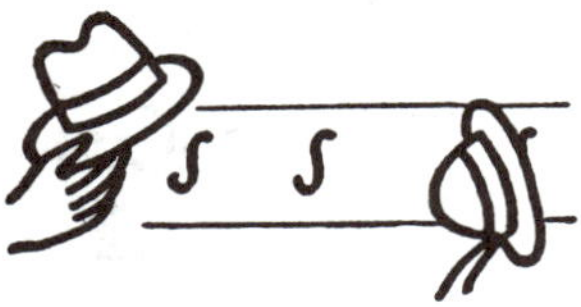

She will put it on a hook with the other hat.

She put it on the hook.

Now it is with the other hat.
The other hat is one of Mary's hats.

John is coming into the room again.

He came into the room.
He went to the table.

He is there now.

The hat is not on the table.

He is saying

"Where is my hat? It is not on my head. It isn't here."

"It isn't (is not) here."

"Where is it? Mary, where is my hat? Where are you, Mary?"

Here is Mary. She is coming into the room.
She says, "Here I am."

isn't ['iznt]

"Where is your hat?"

"You put it on the table. It was on the table."

"I took it. I put it in the other room."

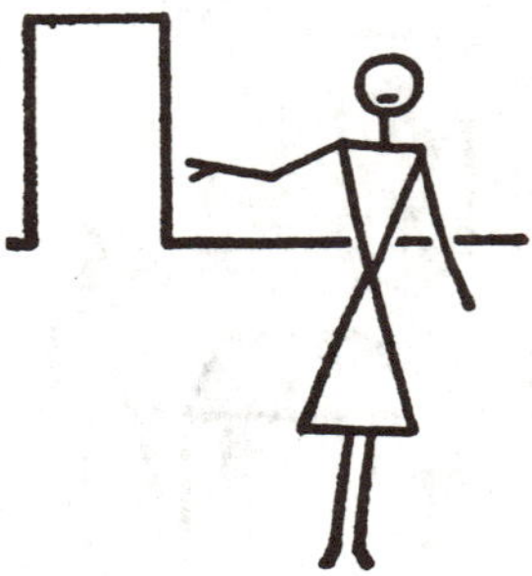

"It is on a hook there. You will see it there."

John says, "I will get my hat."

He is getting it.

Did he get it? Yes. He has it.

He went out of the room.

says [sez]
will get [wəl'get]

is getting [iz'getiŋ]

When he saw the hat he took it off the hook.

He came into the room again with the hat in his hands.
He got it.

He is giving the hat to Mary.

got [gɔt]

What is in the hat?
Mary will see.

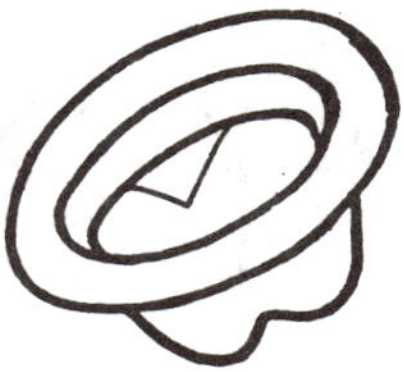

What is she taking from the hat?

What is that in her hand?
It is money.

money [ˈmʌni]

sees [si:z]

What does she see?
One thousand dollars.

The money is in her hand.
It was in the hat.

Where was the hat?
It was on the table.

What did she see?
She saw the hat.
She did not see the money.

She put the hat in the other room.
John went there and got it.

Who got it? John did.

Does she see the money now?
Yes, she sees it.

thousand [ˈθauzənd]

dollars [ˈdɔləz]

I was in the street.
I was coming here.

The wind came. It took my hat off.

I went after my hat.

When I took it up, there was this money.

wind [wind]

up [ʌp]

The money was under the hat.

The hat was over the money.

The wind came. My hat went up.
When the wind came, my hat went up.

The hat came down again.

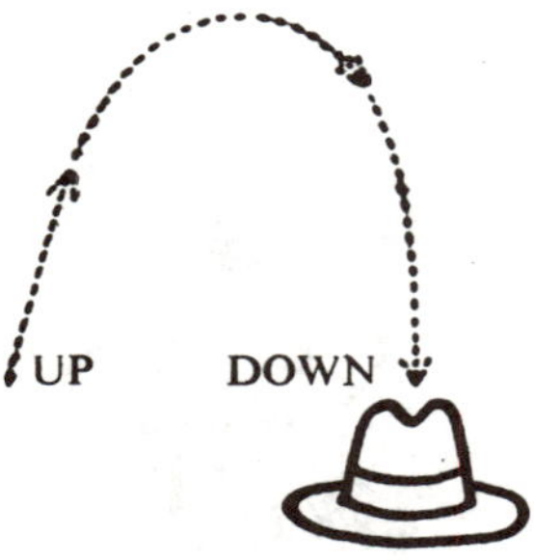

It was over the money.
The money was under the hat.

down [daun]

What is Mary doing?

She is taking things from a drawer.

What are those things in the drawer?

They are knives, forks and spoons.

The drawer has knives, forks and spoons in it.

Mary has a knife, a fork and a spoon in her right hand.

She took them from the drawer.
She will put them on the table.

These are drawers.
One of them is open.
The other two drawers are shut.

doing [ˈduiŋ]
drawer [drɔ:ə*]
knives [naivz]
forks [fɔ:ks]

spoons [spu:nz]
knife [naif]
fork [fɔ:k]
spoon [spu:n]

Mary is getting the soup.
These are plates of soup.

John is taking the chairs to the table.

Mary is on her chairs at the table.

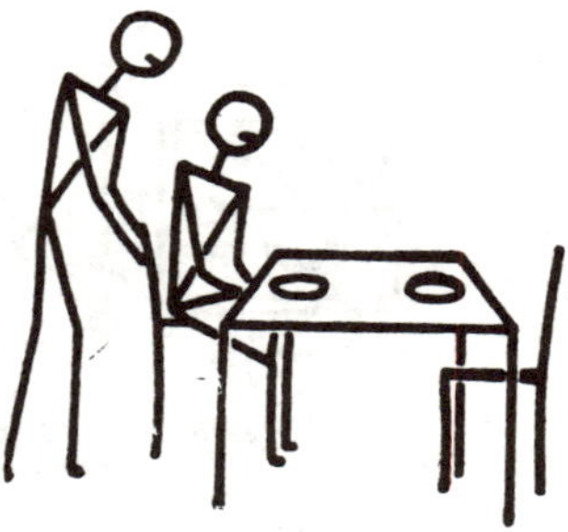

John is on his chairs.
They are on their chairs at the table.

soup [su:p]
plates [pleits]

their [ðɛə*]

Now they are taking their soup.

They have their spoons in their hands.

John is saying to Mary, "I took the hat up."

Mary is saying to John, "Where did the money come from?"

John said, "I saw it there under the hat."
Mary said, "But who put it there?"

John said, "Nobody put it there. The money was there and the wind came and put the hat down over the money."

Nobody = no man or woman or boy or girl or baby.

nobody [ˈnoubədi]

new [nju:]
dress [dres]

old [ould]
pipe [paip]

Mary is getting the new dress. She is in a shop.
The other woman has two dresses in her hands.

This is the shop.

Dresses and hats and shoes are in the window of the shop.

These are shoes.
They are women's shoes.

These are stockings.

These are gloves.
Dresses and stockings and shoes and gloves are clothes.

shop [ʃɔp]
dresses [ˈdresiz]
clothes [klɔ:ðz]

shoes [ʃu:z]
stockings [ˈstɔkiŋz]
gloves [glʌvz]

This is a tree.

This is a branch of the tree.

An apple is on this branch.

It is over the girl's head.

She will take the apple from the branch.
She will put her hand up.

She put her hand up.
She took the apple. It is in her hand.
She took the apple which is in her hand.
She has it in her hand.

She is putting it in her basket.

She put it in her basket.
She had it in her hand before she put it in her basket.
It was on the branch before she put her hand up and took it.

After she took the apple she put it in the basket.
Then she put her basket down.
The apple was up on the tree.
Now it is down in the basket.

tree [tri:]
branch [brɑ:ntʃ]

apple [ˈæpl]
basket [ˈbɑ:skit]

When was the apple on the branch?
When was it over her head?
It was on the branch before she took it. It was on the branch then.

When did she take it?
She took it after she put her hand up.
She took it then.

When did she put it in the basket?
She put it in the basket after she took it from the branch.

When did she have the apple in her hand?
She had it in her hand after she took it from the branch and before she put it in the basket.

This is a box.

This is the front of the box.

This is the back of the box.

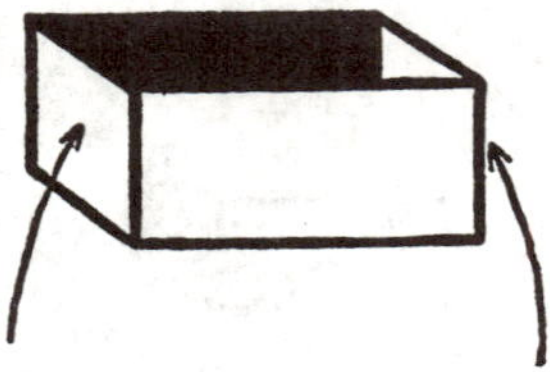

And these are the sides of the box.

This is a house.

This is the front of the house.
This is the front door.

This is a coat.

This is the front of the coat.

box [bɔks]
front [frʌnt]
back [bæk]

sides [saidz]
coat [kout]

These are the arms of the coat.

These are the sides of the coat.

And this is the back of the coat.

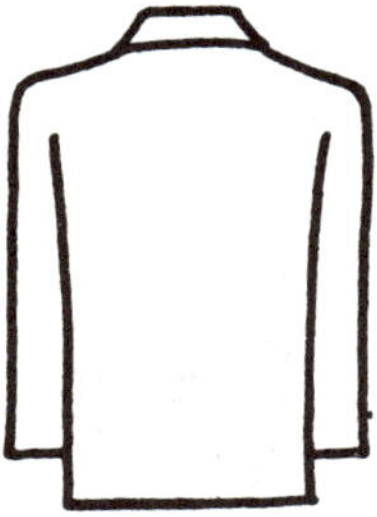

These are a man's arms.

These are his sides.

And this is his back.

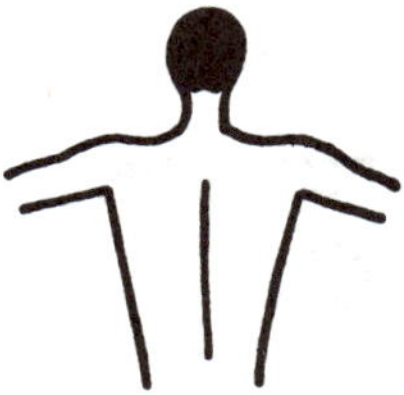

Who is this?
This is Mrs. Smith.
She is Mary Smith.
"Mary Smith" is her name.

What is that? What is in her hands?
It is a tray.
She has a tray in her hands.

She will put the tray on the table.

She is putting the tray on the table.

tray [trei]

She put the tray on the table.

It was in her hands.
It is on the table now.

These are glasses.

What are these?
They are forks.

What is this?
It is a knife.

What are these?
They are two other knives.

Here is the tray.

What are these things on the tray?

What are these?
They are spoons.

What is this?
It is another spoon.

What is this?
It is a plate.

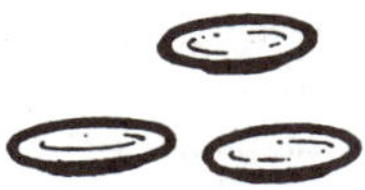

These are three other plates.

Mrs. Smith is taking a knife and fork off the tray.
She has them in her hands.

She is putting them on the table.

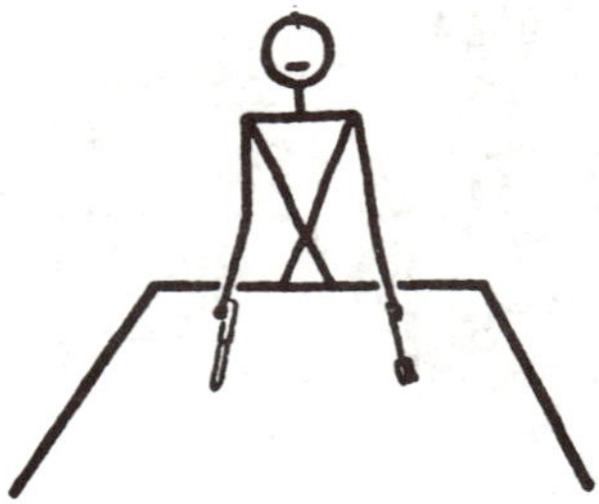

Now she is putting the plates on the table.

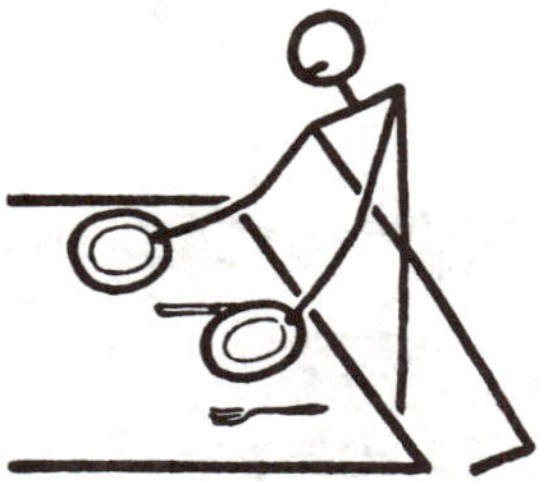

She put the knives and forks and spoons and plates and glasses on the table.
She put these things on the table.

Mary Smith will go from the table to the door.

She is going to the door.
The door is shut.

She went out of the room.
The door is open now.
It was shut.

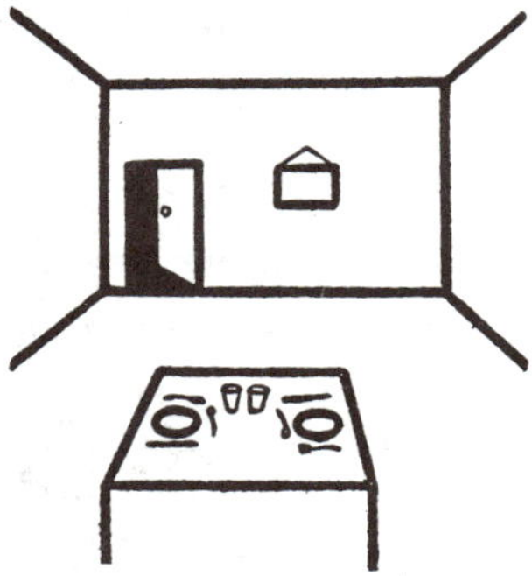

Mary Smith is not in the room.
She was in the room.
She went out of the room.

What is this?
It is a knife.

What is this?

What is this?

What is this?

What are these?

What are these?

What is this?

What is this?

What is this?

What is this?

What is this?

What is this?

What is this?

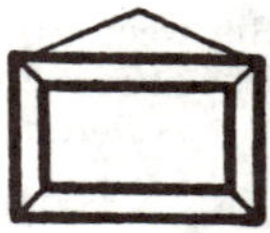

What are these things?

Mary is making soup.

This is a plate of soup.

She will make the soup from milk and potatoes.

These are potatoes.

This is a bottle of milk.
It is cow's milk.

This is a cow.

Cows are animals.
These are some other animals.

a pig

a sheep

a horse

We get milk from cows.
Mary is putting some milk in a cup.

The milk is going into the cup.

is making [iz'meikiŋ]
milk [milk]
potatoes [pə'teitouz]
cow [kau]
animal ['ænimәl]

pig [pig]
sheep [ʃi:p]
horse [hɔ:s]
some [səm]
cup [kʌp]

Mary has a potato in her hand.

She is taking its peel off with a knife.

We get potatoes from the roots of a plant.

Here they are in the earth.

We get them up with a pitchfork.

This is a plant.

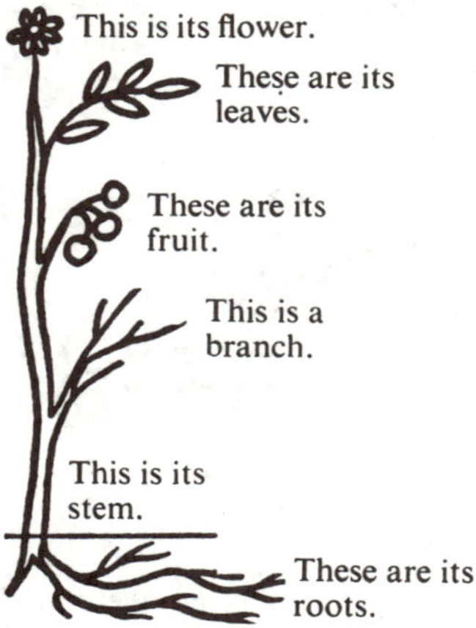

These are roots of other plants.

potato [pə'teitou]
peel [pi:l]
roots [ru:ts]
pitchfork ['pitʃfɔ:k]
earth [ə:θ]

plant [plɑ:nt]
flower ['flauə*]
leaves [li:vz]
fruit [fru:t]
stem [stem]

Mary is making the soup.

This is the saucepan.

This is the lid of the saucepan.

She will make the soup in this saucepan.

She put the potatoes in the saucepan.
The water in the saucepan is boiling.

This is steam.

The saucepan is over the flame.
The flame is under the saucepan.

This is a flame.

saucepan [ˈsɔ:spən]
lid [lid]
is boiling [izˈbɔiliŋ]

steam [sti:m]
flame [fleim]

This water is boiling.
It is giving off steam.
The heat of the flame is making it give off steam.

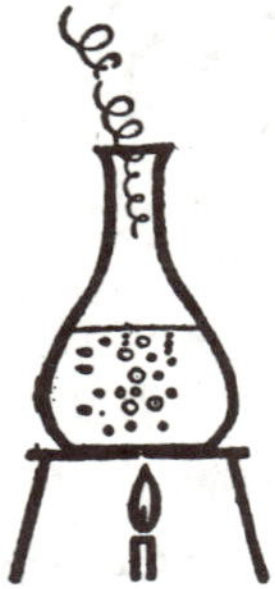

Ice is solid.

This is ice.

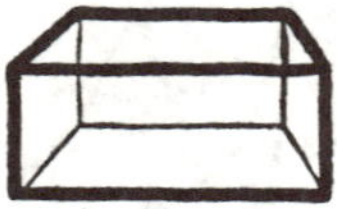

Water is a liquid.
This is water.

This is a tray.
It is a tray of ice.

Ice
is
cold.

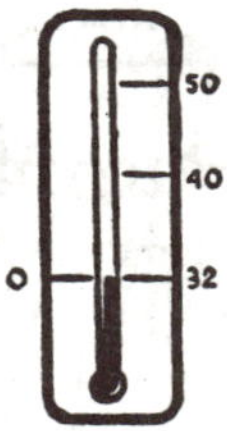

The room is warm.
The heat of the flame is making the room warm.
The things in the room are warm.
Ice is not warm. It is cold.

is giving off [iz'giviŋ'ɔf]
heat [hi:t]
give off ['giv'ɔf]
ice [ais]

solid ['sɔlid]
liquid ['likwid]
cold [kould]
warm [wɔ:m]

This is a bird.
It is on a tree.

The other birds are not on the tree.
They are in the air.

This is a plane.
It is in the air.
It is an aeroplane.
It is going through the air.

These are aeroplanes.

We take in air through our mouths and through our noses.

The air comes in. Then it goes out. That is a breath.

in	out	
		one breath
in	out	two breaths
in	out	

The air is coming out. It is warm.
When it comes out it is warm.

Put your hand here. Your breath is warm.

birds [bə:dz]
the [ði]
air [εə*]
plane [plein]

aeroplane ['εərəplein]
breath [breθ]
breaths [breθs]
comes [kʌmz]

The room is warm.
The water in the saucepan is very warm.
It is boiling.

The air over the flame is very warm.
It goes up.

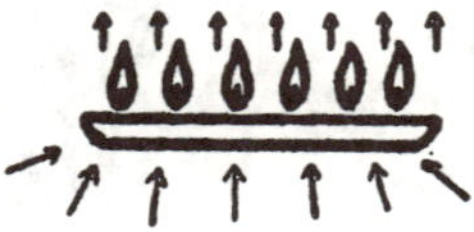

The air under the flame is not very warm. It goes up to the flame.

This is the refrigerator.
It has ice in it.
The air in the refrigerator is cold.

This is the refrigerator.
Mary keeps the milk in the refrigerator.
She keeps it in the cold air.
The air in the refrigerator is cold.
The cold air keeps the milk cold.

very [ˈveri]
goes [gouz]
refrigerator [riˈfridʒəreitə*]

eggs [egz]
keeps [ki:ps]

This is a clock.

A clock is an instrument for measuring time.

This is an instrument for measuring heat.

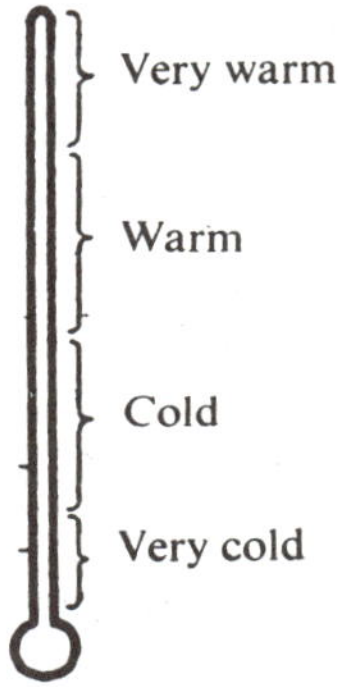

This is a rule.
It is a yard rule.

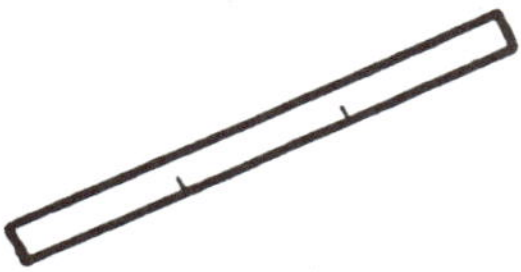

There are three feet in a yard.

There are twelve inches in a foot.

This is
Mary's foot.

These are her feet.

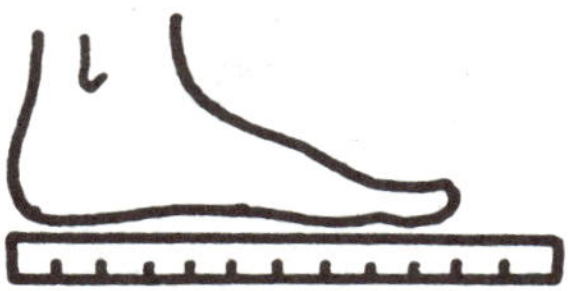

This is John's foot.
It is ten inches long.

instrument [ˈinstrumənt]
for [fə*]
measuring [ˈmeʒəriŋ]

rule [ru:l]
yard [jɑ:d]
inches [ˈintʃiz]

The walls and floor of the refrigerator are thick.

This is a thin line.

This is a thick line.

The thick walls keep the heat of the room out of the refrigerator. They keep the heat from the milk.
The cold air in the refrigerator keeps the milk good.

John is having a drink.
He is having a drink of milk from a glass.

The milk is good.
John is happy.

This milk is not good.
It is bad.

John is not happy.

thick [θik]
thin [θin]
line [lain]
keep [ki:p]

good [gud]
drink [driŋk]
happy [ˈhæpi]
bad [bæd]

This is meat.

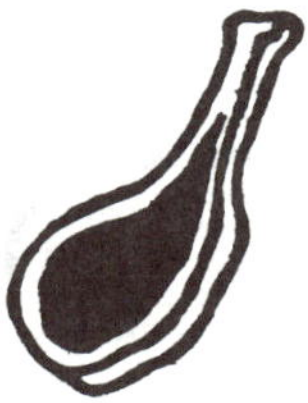

Mary keeps the meat in the refrigerator.

This is bread.

Mary does not keep the bread in the refrigerator.
She keeps it in a bread-bin.

This is cheese.

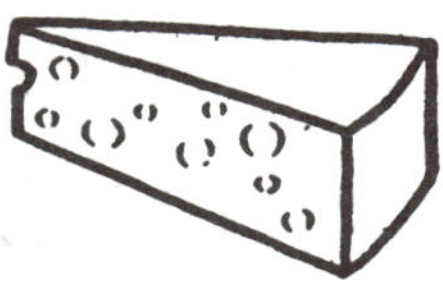

We make cheese from milk.
We get milk from cows.

This is butter.

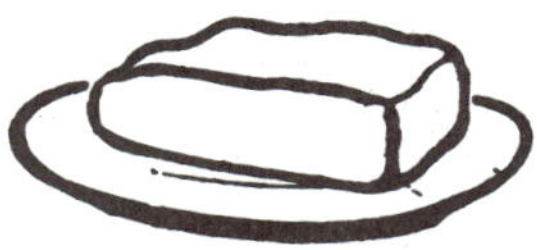

We make butter from milk.
Mary keeps the butter with the milk in the refrigerator.
She keeps the cheese there.

meat [mi:t]
bread [bred]
bread-bin [ˈbred-bin]

cheese [tʃi:z]
butter [ˈbʌtə*]

These are apples.

These are oranges.

Apples and oranges are fruit.
Does Mary keep the fruit in the refrigerator?

What is the time?

It is five-thirty (5:30).
Mary is making the soup.
The potatoes are in the saucepan.
The water in the saucepan is boiling.

What is the time?

The time is five (5:00).
It is five.
Mary will make the soup.

It is five-forty (5:40).

Mary has a fork in her hand.

She is putting the fork into the potatoes.

oranges [ˈɔrindʒiz]
will make [wəlˈmeik]

thirty [ˈθə:ti]
forty [ˈfɔ:ti]

The potatoes are hard.
The fork does not go into them.

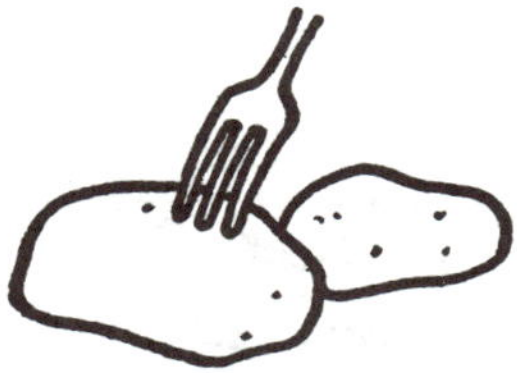

It is five-fifty (5:50).
Mary is putting the fork in again.
She is doing it again.

The potatoes are soft.
The fork goes into them.

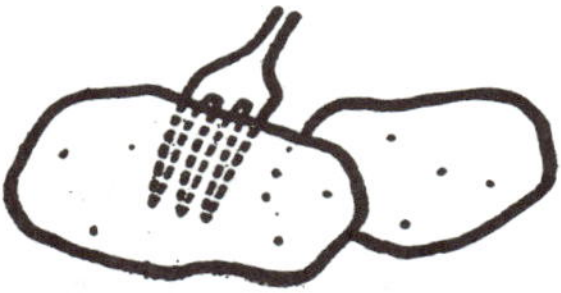

She is taking them out of the saucepan and putting them on a plate.

hard [hɑ:d]
fifty [ˈfifti]

soft [sɔft]

The potatoes are on the plate.

They were in the saucepan.
They were hard.
They are soft now.

Mary is crushing them with a fork.

They are not hard now.
They are soft.

Bread is soft.

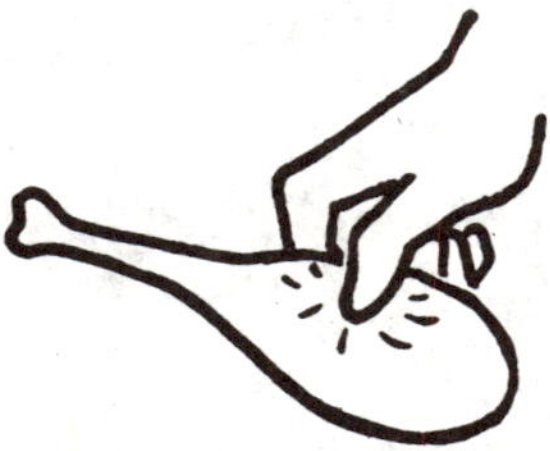

Meat is soft.

Glass is hard.

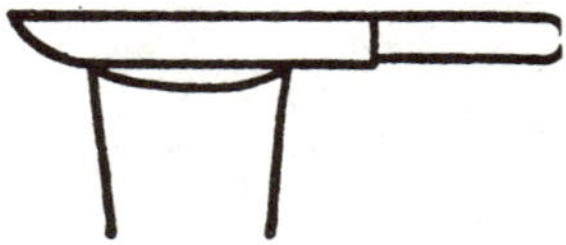

Butter is soft.

is crushing [iz'krʌʃiŋ]

John has a bit of cheese in his fingers.

He is putting the bit of cheese in his mouth.

Now it is between his teeth.

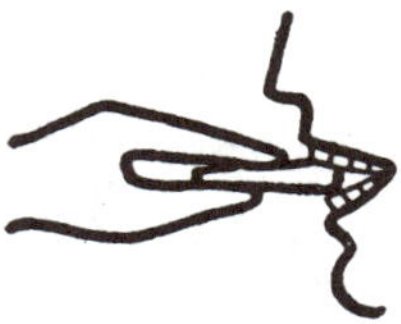

This is his mouth.

This is a tooth.

These are teeth.

The cheese is not soft.

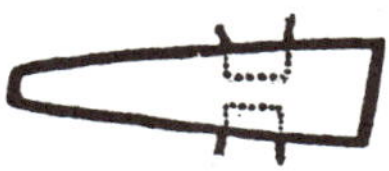

It is hard.

John's teeth do not go into the cheese.

a bit of [ə'bitəv]
teeth [ti:θ]

tooth [tu:θ]

Mary put the potatoes and the milk and other things into the saucepan.
This is salt.
(See page 242.)

She put the saucepan over a low flame.
She put the lid on the saucepan.

The low flame is under the saucepan.

This flame is low.

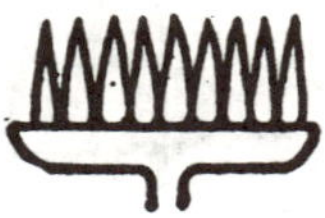

This flame is high.

This building is high.

This building is low.

salt [sɔ:lt]
low [lou]

high [hai]
building [ˈbildiŋ]

What is the time?
It is six (6:00).

Mary is tasting the soup.
It has a good taste.
The soup is ready.

Now she is putting the soup in the plates.

It was in the saucepan.

Now it is in the plates.

She made the soup.
She put it in the plates.
She took them to the table.

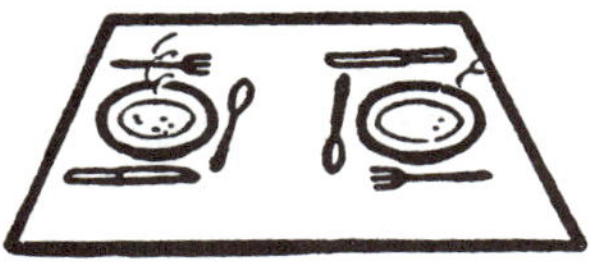

The plates are on the table.
The soup is ready.
It is good soup.
Mary made it.

is tasting [iz'teistiŋ]
taste [teist]

ready ['redi]
made [meid]

Soup, apples, butter,

potatoes, oranges, bread,

meat, cheese, milk

are food.

They are different sorts of food.

These are different sorts of glasses.

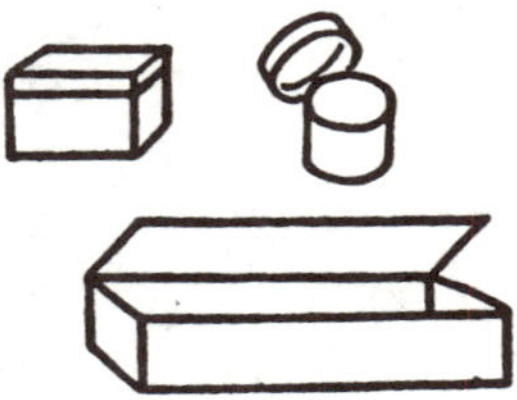

These are different sorts of boxes.

Apples and oranges are different sorts of fruit.

An apple

An orange

Glasses and boxes and fingers and dresses and flames are things. They are different sorts of things.

food [fu:d]
different [ˈdifrənt]

sorts [sɔ:ts]
orange [ˈɔrindʒ]

Cows

and sheep

and pigs

and horses

and goats

are animals.

They are different sorts of animals.

These are the same.

These are different.

These are the same.

These are different.

goats [gouts]
leaf [li:f]

These are different sorts of plants.

This is the leaf of one sort of plant.

This is the leaf of another sort of plant.

These plates are the same.

These plates are different.

These glasses are the same.

These are different. 

sort [sɔ:t]
the same [ðə'seim]

Here are a woman and a boy.

The boy is the woman's son.
She is his mother.
He is her son.

Here are a woman and a girl.

The girl is the woman's daughter.
The woman is her mother.

Here are a man and his son.

The man is the father of the boy.
He is the boy's father.

Here are a man and his daughter.

He is the father of the girl.
He is the girl's father.
She is his daughter.

son [sʌn]
mother ['mʌðə*]

daughter ['dɔ:tə*]
father ['fɑ:ðə*]

The boy is the brother of the girl.

He is the girl's brother.
He is her brother.

The girl is the sister of the boy.
She is the boy's sister.
She is his sister.

This man and woman

have
two sons

This boy has one brother and three sisters.

This girl has two brothers and two sisters.
They are a family of seven (7).

and
three daughters.

brother [ˈbrʌðə*]
sister [ˈsistə*]
sons [sʌnz]
daughters [ˈdɔ:təz]

sisters [ˈsistəz]
brothers [ˈbrʌðəz]
family [ˈfæmili]

Here are Mrs. Smith,
her daughter Jane,
and her son Tom.

They are at the table.
They are having their potato soup.

Potato soup is a thick soup. It is not clear.
Thick soup and clear soup are two different sorts of soup.

This water is clear. When a liquid is clear we see through it.

Milk is not a clear liquid. We do not see through it.

The air is clear. I see the mountains.
When the air is not clear
I do not see them.

Jane [dʒein]
Tom [tɔm]

clear [kliə*]
mountains [ˈmauntinz]

This soup is clear. We see the spoon through it.

Potato soup is a thick soup. We do not see the spoon through it.

Who is this?

This is Mary Smith.
She made the soup.
This is Mary who made the soup.

This is the soup. Mary made it.
This is the soup which Mary made.

This is the milk. Mary put it in the soup.
This is the milk which Mary put in the soup.

This is a spoon. It is in my hand.
This is a spoon which is in my hand.

That is a glass of water. It is on the table.
That is a glass of water which is on the table.

This is a bone. It was in the dog's mouth.
This is a bone which was in the dog's mouth.

This is a dog. He had the bone.

This is the dog who had it.

bone [boun]

QUESTIONS

a What is the time?

b What are these?

c What is this?

d What are these?

e What are these?

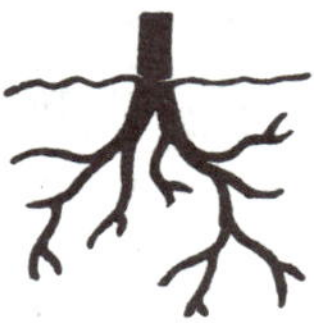

f What is this?

g What is this?

h What is this?

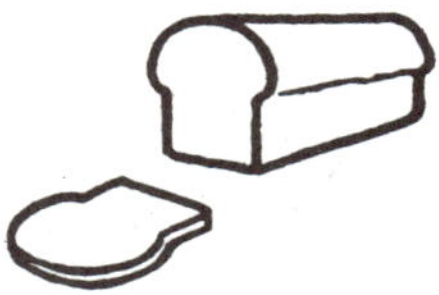

116 [wʌnˈhʌndrədˈsiksˈtiːn]

Answers are on page 116.

QUESTIONS

a What is this?

b What is this?

c What are these?

d What is this?

e What is this?

f What are these?

g What is this?

h What is this?

Answers are on page 116.

a This is a family.

What do you see?

b This is a plant.

Which parts of the plant do you see?

c This is a refrigerator.

What do you see in it?

d This is a dog.

Which parts of the dog do you see?

e What do you see?

f What do you see?

g What do you see?

h What do you see?

Answers are on page 116.

Answers to questions on pages 113-115.

Page 113

a The time is four-forty-two (4:42).
c It is a saucepan.
e They are roots.
g It is butter.

b They are apples.
d They are leaves.
f It is a bottle of milk.
h It is bread.

Page 114

a It is cheese.
c They are flames.
e It is a high building.
g It is a pig.

b It is a cup.
d It is a horse.
f They are a box and its lid.
h It is a sheep.

Page 115

a I see a father and mother and their son and daughter.
c I see a bottle of milk and four eggs and two roots.
e I see a bone. It is on the floor. And I see the leg of a table.
g I see a woman. She has a spoon in her hand. She is tasting the soup.

b I see its roots and its stem and its leaves and its flower.
d I see its head and ears and nose, its body, its legs, and its tail.
f I see two glasses. One of them has liquid in it.
h I see a man. He has a glass in his hand. He is having a drink from the glass.

---

113 [wʌnˈhʌndredˈθəːˈtiːn]

115 [wʌnˈhʌndredˈfifˈtiːn]

a Where are the women?
What has one woman in her hands?

b What are these?

c What is the girl doing?

Where is the apple?

d Where will she put the apple?
Where was it before she took it?
(See pages 82-83.)

e What are some different sorts of food?

f What are some different sorts of animals?

g What are some different sorts of fruits?

h What are some different sorts of persons?

Answers are on page 120.

82 [ˈeitiˈtu:]
83 [ˈeitiˈθri:]

120 [wʌnˈhʌndrəd əndˈtwenti]

a This is a glass of milk. Is it clear? Do you see through it?

b Is the glass in this window clear? What do you see through the window?

c Is glass hard?
e Is ice warm?

d Is meat soft?
f Are flames cold?

g What is he doing?

h What is she doing?

121 [wʌnˈhʌndrəd ənd ˈtwenti ˈwʌn]

Answers are on page 121.

a What do you see?

b What is he doing?

c What are they doing?

d What are these?

e What do we keep in the refrigerator?

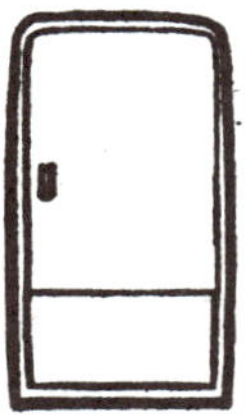

f What are some different sorts of things? Give the names of ten different things which you see in a house.

Answers are on page 121.

Answers to questions on page 117.

Page 117

a They are in a shop. It is a clothes shop. She has two dresses in her hands.

b These are shoes (women's shoes) and stockings and gloves.

c The girl is putting her hand up to the apple. It is on a branch of an apple tree.

d She will put it in her basket. Before she took the apple it was on the tree.

e Bread, butter, milk, cheese, meat, eggs, and fruit are different sorts of food.

f Cows, pigs, sheep, goats, and horses are different sorts of animals.

g Apples and oranges are different sorts of fruit.

h Men, women, boys, girls, and babies are different sorts of persons.

117 [wʌnˈhʌndrəd ənd ˈsevnˈti:n]

Answers to questions on pages 118-119.

Page 118

a No, it is not clear.
No, I do not see through it.

b Yes. The glass in the window is clear. I see some mountains and a house.

c Yes. Glass is hard.

d Yes. Some meat is soft. But some meat is hard.

e No. Ice is cold.

f No. Flames are not cold.

g He is taking potatoes out of the earth with a pitchfork.

h She is putting some salt in the potato soup.

Page 119

a I see a man. He is in a street. His hat is in the air. The wind is taking it up. The wind took it off his head.

b He is putting his hat on his head.

c They are on their chairs at the table. They have their spoons in their hands. They are taking their soup.

d One of them is a clock. The other is an instrument for measuring heat.

e We keep the milk, butter, cheese, eggs, meat and fruit in the refrigerator.

f Rooms and doors and windows and tables and chairs and boxes and knives and spoons and forks and shelves... are different sorts of things.

118 [wʌnˈhʌndrəd ənd ˈeiˈti:n]

119 [wʌnˈhʌndrəd ənd ˈnainˈti:n]

This is a bedroom.
There are two beds in it.

This chair is by the bed.

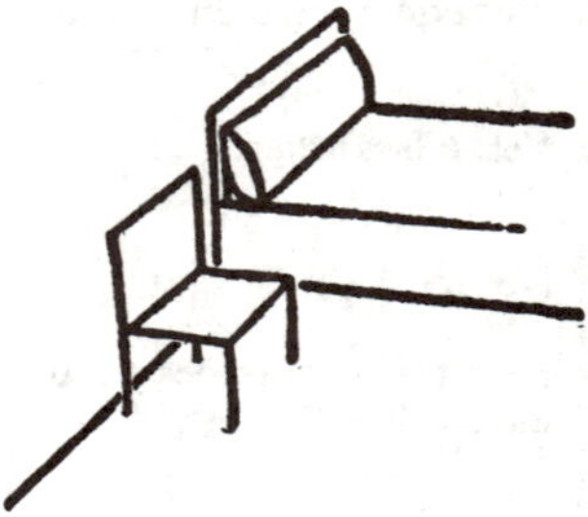

What is on the chair?
A bag is on the chair.

A woman is by the bed.
Who is she?
She is Mrs. Smith.

bedroom [ˈbedrum]
bed [bed]

by [bai]
bag [bæg]

What is she doing?
She is putting things into the bag.

What is she putting into the bag?
She is putting Mr. Smith's things into it.

Mr. Smith is going to California. Mr. and Mrs. Smith are in New York State.

He will go by train. This is a train. From New York State to California is a long journey.

California [kæli'fɔ:njə]
New York State ['nju:'jɔ:k 'steit]

train [trein]
journey ['dʒə:ni]

What will he take with him to California?
He will take some shirts.

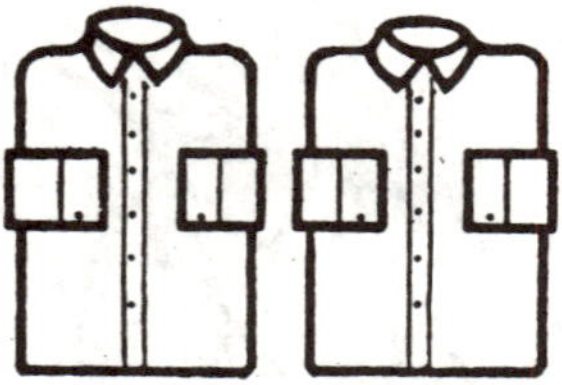

He will take some socks.

He will not take old socks. Old socks have holes in them.

He will take new socks.
New socks have no holes in them.

These trousers have a hole in them.
They are old trousers.

shirts [ʃə:ts]
socks [sɔks]
holes [houlz]

trousers [ˈtrauzəz]
hole [houl]

He will take some shoes.

He will put them in a shoe bag.

My hands are dirty.

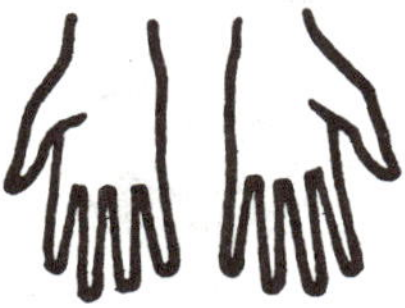

My hands are clean.

shoe bag [ˈʃuːˈbæg]
clean [kliːn]
shirt [ʃəːt]

The shoe bag will keep the other things clean.

The bag is between the shoes and the shirt. The shoes will not make the shirt dirty.

This cloth is dirty.

This cloth is clean.

dirty [ˈdəːti]
cloth [klɔθ]

This plate is clean.

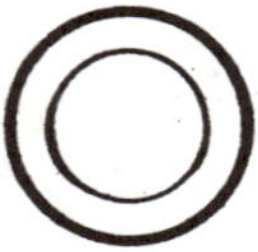

This plate is dirty.

His face is dirty.

His face is clean.

The plate is dirty but the cloth is clean.

Now the cloth is dirty but the plate is clean.

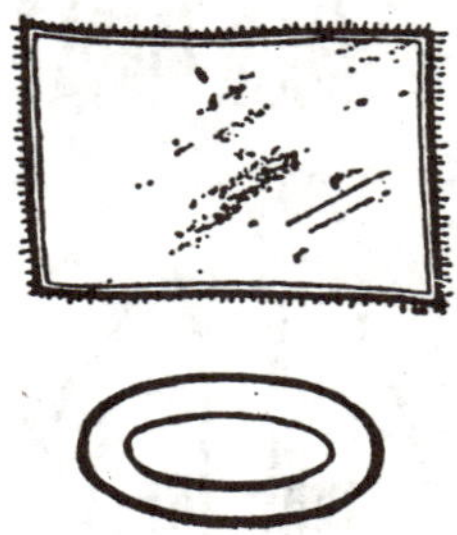

This is a basin.

This is warm water in it.

This is soap.

What is she doing?

She is washing her hands with soap and warm water.

Her hands are wet now but they are clean. They were dirty.

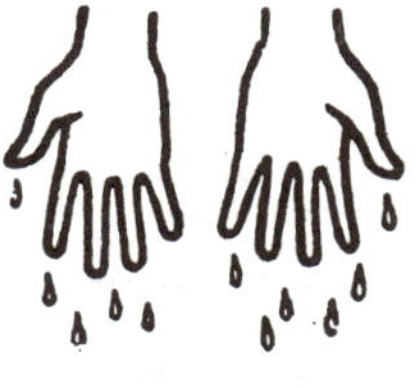

basin [ˈbeisn]
soap [soup]

is washing [izˈwɔʃiŋ]
wet [wet]

What is she doing?
She is drying her hands on a cloth.
This cloth is a towel

Her hands were wet.

Now they are dry.
They were dirty.
Now they are clean.

What is this?
It is a brush.
It is a toothbrush.

What is this?
It is toothpaste.

She is putting some toothpaste on the brush.

is drying [iz'draiiŋ]
towel ['tauəl]
dry [drai]

brush [brʌʃ]
toothbrush ['tu:θbrʌʃ]
toothpaste ['tu:θpeist]

Now she is brushing her teeth.

Her teeth will be clean.
They will be clean and white.

What is this?
It is a comb.

And this?

It is a brush.
It is a hairbrush.

She is brushing her hair.

Now she is combing her hair.

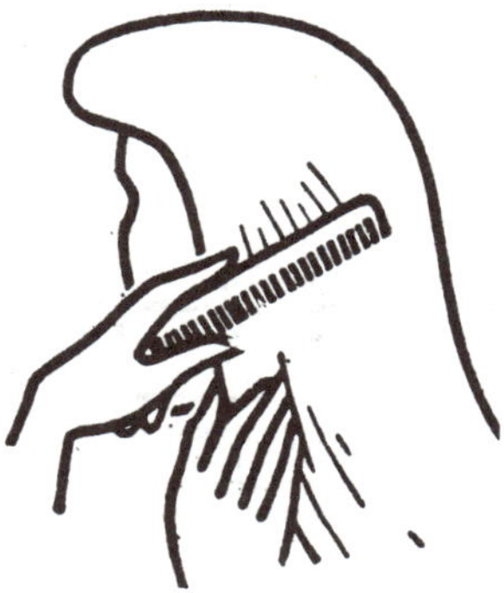

is brushing [iz'brʌʃiŋ]
white [wait]
comb [koum]

hairbrush ['hɛəbrʌʃ]
is combing [iz'koumiŋ]

What are these?

They are pins.

This pin

is like this pin.

One pin is very like another pin.

But they are two pins.
They are not the same pin. They are different pins.

These are three hairpins.
They are different hairpins.

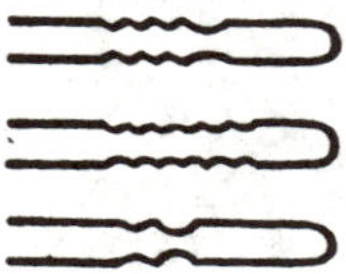

She has a hairpin in her hand.
She is putting it in her hair.

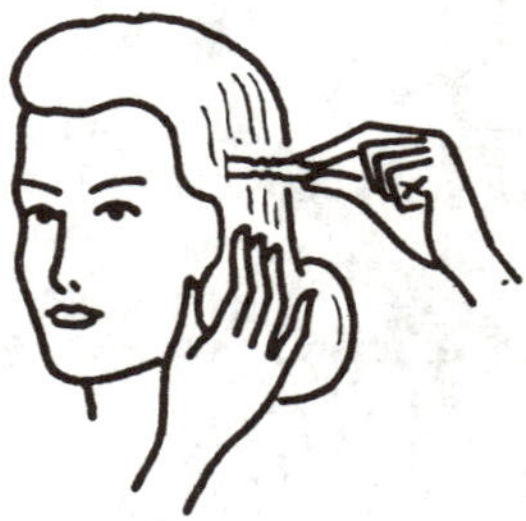

pins [pinz]
like [laik]
pin [pin]

hairpins [ˈhɛəpinz]
hairpin [ˈhɛəpin]

Now it is in her hair.
It was in her hand.
It is in her hair now.
But it is the same hairpin.

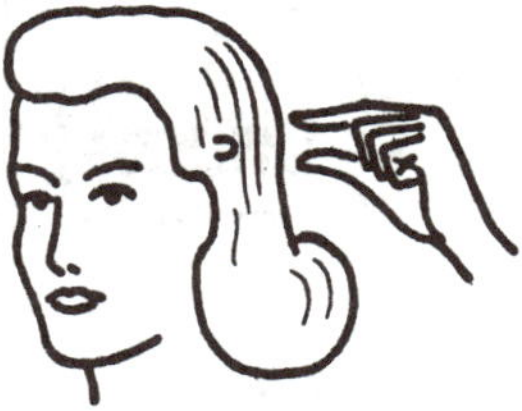

He is brushing his hair.
He does not put pins in his hair.

Mrs. Smith put some shirts and some socks and shoes (in a shoe bag) and a comb and brushes and toothpaste and soap and a towel in Mr. Smith's bag.

She put all these things in his bag.

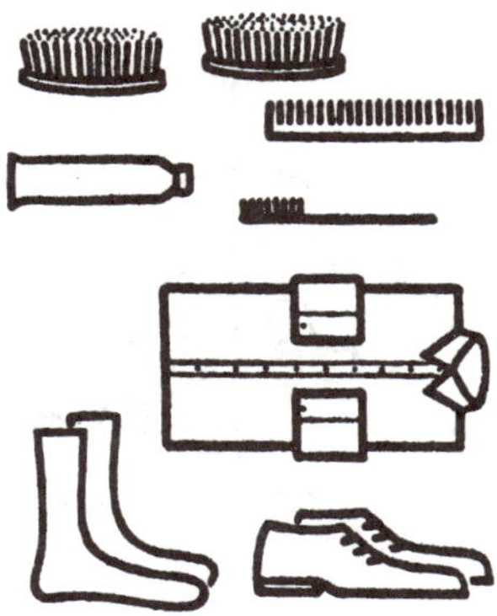

Mr. Smith will go to the station in a taxi.

This is a taxi.
Mr. Smith is getting into it.
He has his bag with him.

This is the station.
The taxi is in front of the station.
The time is 8:00.
The train will go at 8:30.

Mr. Smith is getting out of the taxi.

Now he is going into the station.

station [ˈsteiʃən]
taxi [ˈtæksi]

in front of [inˈfrʌntəv]

This is the waiting room in the station.

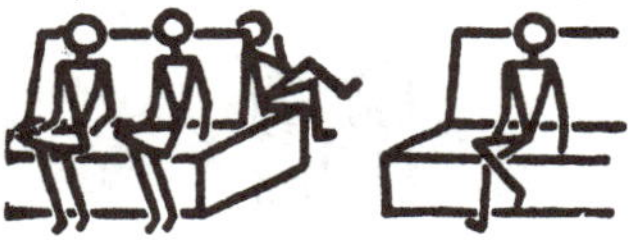

Those men and women on the seats in the waiting room are waiting. They are waiting for their trains.

These are rails. The train goes on these rails.
It is a railway train.

Here is a train.

This is the engine of a train.

This is the bell on the engine.

Here is the ticket office in the station.
Mr. Smith got his ticket here.

waiting room [ˈweitiŋrum]
are waiting [ɑ:ˈweitiŋ]
engine [ˈendʒin]
bell [bel]

rails [reilz]
railway [ˈreilwei]
tickets [ˈtikits]
ticket office [ˈtikitˈɔfis]

Here is his ticket.
He gave $ 132.35 for his ticket.

These are tickets.

How long is the journey?
Four days.
Which days will he be on the train?
He will be on the train Sunday, Monday, Tuesday, Wednesday.
The other days of the week are Thursday, Friday, Saturday.

How much was his ticket for the journey to Los Angeles?
It was one hundred and thirty-two dollars and thirty-five cents ($ 132.35).

How much money did he take with him for his journey?
He took five hundred and nineteen dollars ($ 519.00).
Much money: $ 5000
Little money: $ 5.

$132.35 [wʌnˈhundred ˈθɔ:tiˈtuˈdɔləz ˈθɔ:tiˈfaiv ˈsents] · how [hau] · much [mʌtʃ] · Los Angeles [lɔsˈændʒili:z] · days [deiz] · Sunday [ˈsʌndi] · Monday [ˈmʌndi] · Tuesday [ˈtju:zdi] · Wednesday [ˈwenzdi] · week [wi:k] · Thursday [ˈθɔ:zdi] · Friday [ˈfraidi] · Saturday [ˈsætədi] · nineteen [ˈnainˈti:n] $ 5000 [faivˈθauzəndˈdɔləz] · little [ˈlitl]

Mr. Smith has friends in California.

Mr. Smith His friends

Here are his friends.
He and his friends are shaking hands. (See page 254.)

His friends were waiting for him at the station.

They say, "Did you have a good journey?"
He says, "Yes, but it was a long journey."

His friend says, "Let me have your bag, please."
He will go with his friends to their house.

friends [frendz]
are shaking [ɑ:ˈʃeikiŋ]
254 [tuˈhʌndred ənd ˈfiftiˈfɔ:*]

let me have [ˈlet miˈhæv]
please [pli:z]
friend [frend]

This is a letter: *a*.
These are letters: *a*, *b*, *c*.
This is a word: *man*.
Three letters make the word *man*.
The man is writing a letter.
He is writing on paper with a pen.

This is the letter:
It is in Mr. Roe's writing.
Mr. Roe will send the letter to Mr. Doe.

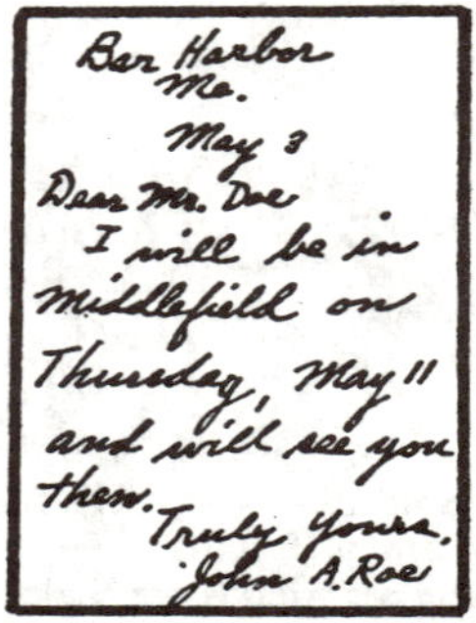

Here is the letter ready for the post

Here is the stamp.

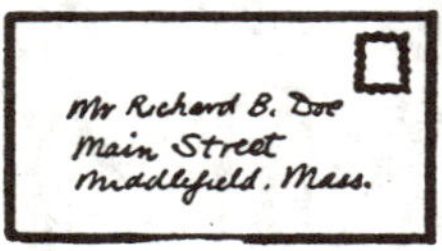

Mr. Doe's name and street and town are on the letter.
Mass. is short for Massachusetts.
Middlefield is in Massachusetts.

This is the back of the letter.
Mr. Roe's name, and the town where he is living are on the back of the letter.

Me. is short for Maine.
Bar Harbor is in Maine.
Massachusetts and Maine are two states of the United States of America.

letter [ˈletə*] · a [ei] · b [bi:] · c [si:] · word [wə:d] · is writing [izˈraitiŋ] · paper [ˈpeipə*] · pen [pen] · Me. (Maine) [mein] · May [mei] · dear [diə*] · May 11 [mei ði iˈlevnθ] · truly [ˈtru:li] · yours [jɔ:z] · will send [wəlˈsend] · post [poust] · stamp [stæmp] · town [taun] · Mass. (Massachusetts) [mæsəˈtʃu:sets] · is living [izˈliviŋ] · state [ˈsteit]

Mr. Smith is writing a card to Mrs. Smith. He is in San Francisco. On one side of the card is a picture of the harbour. Here is the picture.
This is a picture postcard.

Here is the other side of the card. Mr. Smith is putting Mrs. Smith's name on it.
He will put her street under the name.
He will put her town under the street.
Then he will put the state where her town is.

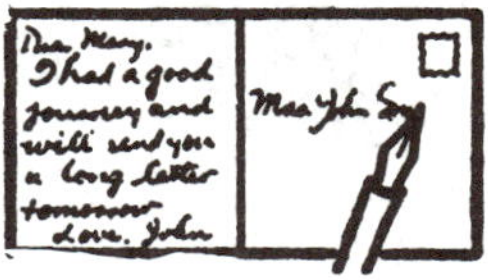

Now the card is ready for the post.
There is a stamp on the card.
Mrs. Smith's name and street and town are on the right hand side of the card.
Mrs. Smith's town is in New York State.

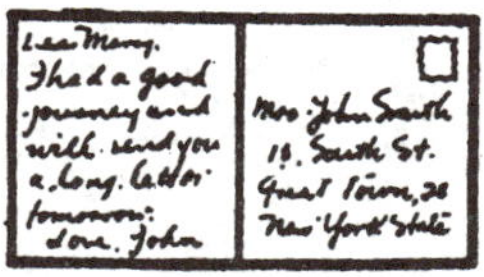

Mr. Smith is taking the card to the Post Office.
He is going up the steps.
He will put the card in the letter box on the wall of the Post Office.
He is sending the card to Mrs. Smith.

card [kɑ:d]
San Francisco [sænfrənˈsiskou]
harbour [ˈhɑ:bə*]
postcard [ˈpoustkɑ:d]

Post Office [ˈpoustɔfis]
steps [steps]
letter box [ˈletəbɔks]

This morning Mrs. Smith got the card which Mr. Smith sent to her from San Francisco.
She is reading it now.
She is reading: "I had a good journey...."

Reading and writing are parts of our education.
We get a great part of our education at school.
These boys and girls are at school. The teacher is teaching them.

Mrs. Smith is sending Jane and Tom to school.
They will be at school before nine.
They get good teaching at school.

At school, Tom and Jane are learning. They were reading and now they are writing.
Tom is writing the word *learning* on the board.
The teacher is teaching him the word *learning*.

morning [ˈmɔ:niŋ]
sent [sent]
is reading [izˈri:diŋ]
education [edjuˈkeiʃən]
great [greit]

school [sku:l]
teacher [ˈti:tʃə*]
is teaching [izˈti:tʃiŋ]
are learning [a:ˈlə:niŋ]
board [bɔ:d]

Now Tom and Jane are back from school. Jane is reading a story.

It is eight-thirty.

Tom is writing at the table.

Tom's dog is at his feet.

Mrs. Smith is reading the newspaper.

Tom and Jane are getting a good education. They get some of it at school, and they get some of it from their mother and father. Mrs. Smith is taking a look at Tom's work. It is good work.

Now Mrs. Smith is writing a letter to Mr. Smith. She sends love from Tom and Jane to their father.

She will send the letter to Mr. Smith.

She has the letter in her hand.

Now she is sending the letter.

She sent the letter.

story [ˈstɔ:ri]
newspaper [ˈnju:speipə*]
is taking a look [izˈteikiŋ əˈluk]

work [wə:k]
love [lʌv]
well [wel]

a What are these?

b What are these?

What is this boy doing?

What is the man doing?

c What are these?

d What is this?

What is the girl doing?

What is the woman doing?

148 [ə'hʌndrəd ənd'fɔ:ti'eit]

Answers are on page 148.

QUESTIONS

a On page 133, where did Mr. Smith get his ticket?

b How much was the ticket?

c How long was the journey to Los Angeles?

d Did he go in an aeroplane?

e What did his friends say to him when they saw him?

f What did he say on the card which he sent to Mrs. Smith?

g What are Tom and Jane learning at school?

h What did Mrs. Smith send to Mr. Smith from Tom and Jane?

133 [əˈhʌndrəd ənd ˈθəːtiˈθriː]

Answers are on page 148.

This is a plate.
The plate is round.

This is an orange.
The orange is round.

The face of
the clock is
round.
The hands of
the clock go round.

This is the moon.

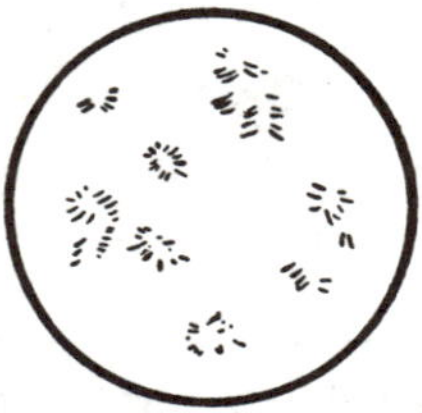

The moon is round.

round [raund]
moon [mu:n]
sun [sʌn]

This is the earth.

The earth is round.

This is the sun.

This is
the sky.

This is a cloud in the sky.

This is the earth.

sky [skai]
cloud [klaud]

The sun comes up in the East.

It comes up every morning.

The sun goes down in the West.

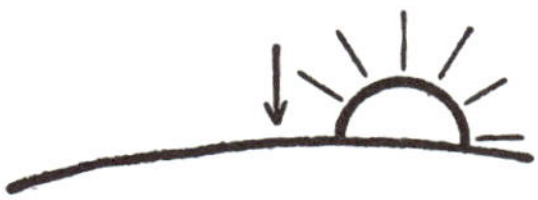

It goes down every night.

What is the time?
It is five-eight a.m.

The sun is coming up now at five-eight (5:08) a.m.

What is the time?
It is five-twenty (5:20) p.m.

The sun is going down now at five-twenty (5:20) p.m.

comes up [ˈkʌmzˈʌp]
East [i:st]
goes down [ˈgouz ˈdaun]
West [west]

every [ˈevri]
night [nait]
a.m. [eiem]
p.m. [pi:em]

Yesterday the sun came up at five-seven (5:07) a.m. and went down at eight-nineteen (8:19) p.m.
Today the sun came up at five-six (5:06) a.m. and will go down at eight-twenty (8:20) p.m.
Tomorrow it will come up at five-five (5:05) a.m. and will go down at eight twenty-one (8:21).

This is night.

This is the earth.
That is a star.

This is morning.

The sun is coming up.

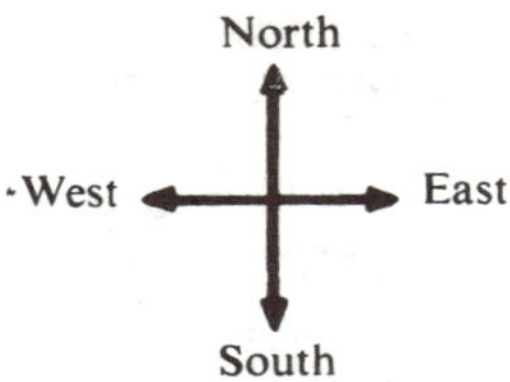

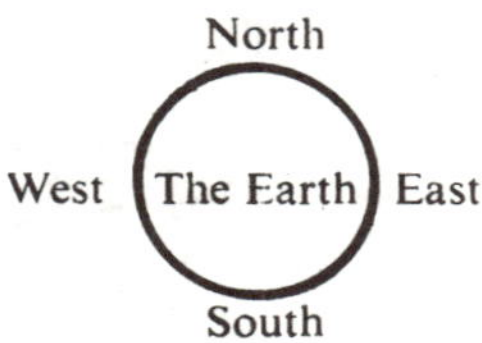

North, South, East, West are four directions.

There are twenty-four hours in one day.
Twenty-four hours make one day.
Two and two make four.
Three and five make eight.
What do five and six make?
Do they make ten, or eleven, or twelve?
That is a question.
The answer is "Eleven".

---

yesterday [ˈjestədi]
today [təˈdei]
tomorrow [təˈmɔrou]
star [stɑ:*]

North [nɔ:θ]
South [sauθ]
directions [diˈrekʃənz]
hours [ˈauəz]

Say these numbers: 1, 2, 3, 4, 5, 6, 7, 8, 9, 10, 11, 12.
What number comes after 12?
Thirteen.
What comes after 13?
Fourteen.
What comes after 14?
Fifteen.

What numbers come after 15?
Sixteen 16
Seventeen 17
Eighteen 18
Nineteen 19
Twenty 20

Twenty 20 Twenty-one 21
Thirty 30 Thirty-one 31
Forty 40 Forty-one 41
Fifty 50 Fifty-one 51
Sixty 60 Seventy 70

Eighty 80 Ninety 90
A hundred 100
A hundred and one 101
A thousand 1000
A million 1,000,000

thirteen ['θə:'ti:n] · fourteen ['fɔ:'ti:n] · fifteen ['fif'ti:n] · sixteen ['siks'ti:n] · seventeen ['sevn'ti:n] · eighteen ['ei'ti:n] · twenty ['twenti] · sixty ['siksti] · seventy ['sevnti] · eighty ['eiti] · ninety ['nainti] · a hundred [ə'hʌndred] · a million [ə'miljən]

Answers are on page 149.

a What do seven and eleven make?
What do twenty and forty make?
What do thirteen and thirty make?
What do two hundred and three and three hundred and four make?

b Where does the sun come up and where does it go down?
Does day come after night?
Does night come after day?

c This is a letter. Where do we put Mr. Green's street and town and state on the letter?

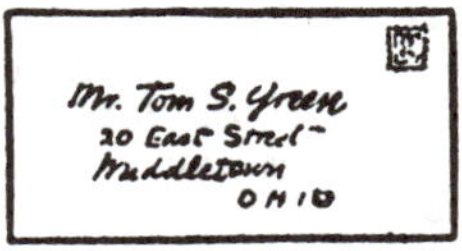

d Tom's work at school is learning. He is a learner. What is the teacher's work?

learner [lə:nə*]

Answers are on page 149.

Answers to questions on pages 140-141.

Page 140

a They are shoes.
He is putting his shoes on his feet.

b They are shirts.
He is putting his things in his bag.

c They are toothpaste and a toothbrush.
She is brushing her teeth.

d It is soap.
She is washing her hands.

Page 141

a He got his ticket at the ticket office in the station.

b The ticket was $ 132.35

c The journey was four days long.

d No. He did not go in an aeroplane. He went in a train.

e They said, "Did you have a good journey?"

f He said, "I had a good journey and will send you a long letter tomorrow. Love. John."

g They are learning reading and writing at school.

h She sent love from Tom and Jane.

Answers to questions on pages 146-147.

Page 146

a	a bed	b	a bag	c	a sock
d	a stocking	e	a shoe	f	a hairbrush
g	a toothbrush	h	a comb	i	a key
j	a lock	k	a hairpin	l	a fork
m	an engine	n	a plate	o	two pins
p	a pen	q	rails	r	a card
s	a stamp	t	a flame	u	a frame
v	a hook	w	a book	x	a bell
y	a bottle	z	a glove		

Page 147

a Eighteen. Sixty. Forty-three. Five hundred and seven.

b The sun comes up in the East and goes down in the West. Yes, day comes after night. Yes, night comes after day.

c We put his street under his name and we put the name of the town under the name of the street. And under that we put the name of the state.

d The teacher's work is teaching.

This boy's name is Tom.

This girl's name is Jane.

Tom is making something.

Jane is saying, "What are you making, Tom?"

something ['sʌmθiŋ]

Tom is saying, "I am making a house."

This is a box.

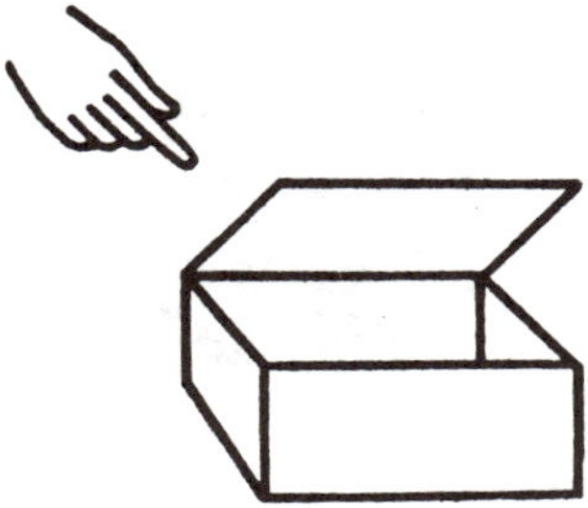

This is one side of the box.

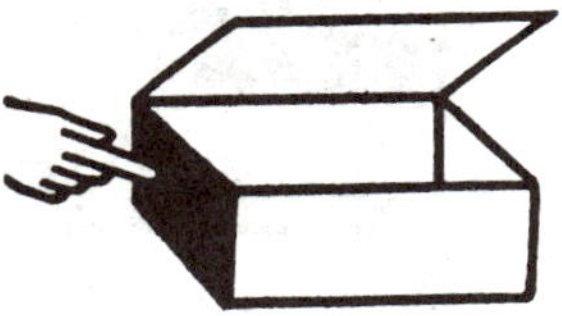

This is the opposite side of the box.

opposite [ˈɔpəzit]

This is the front of the box.

And this is the back of the box.

This is the bottom of the box.

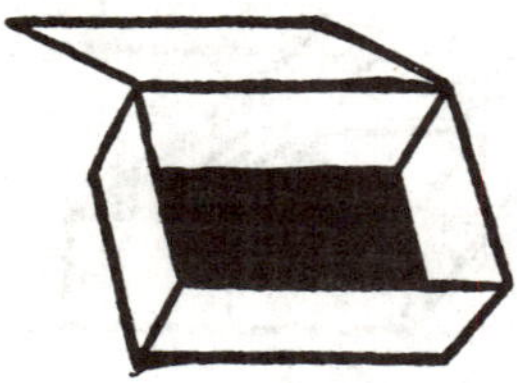

And this is the lid of the box.

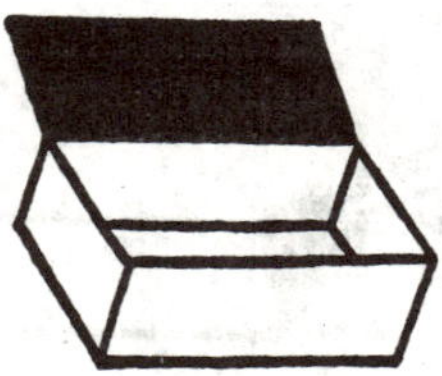

bottom [ˈbɔtəm]

Now this side will be one wall of the house.

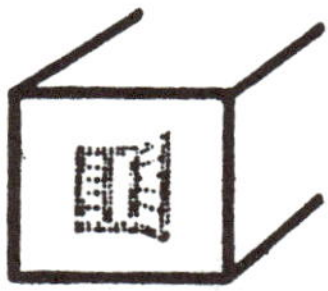

I will put a window in here.

This will be the opposite wall of the house.

I will put another window in this opposite wall.

The front of the box will be the front of the house.

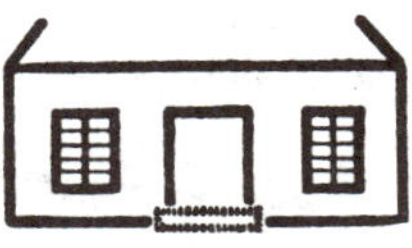

I will put a step under the door.

This is a step.

These are steps — three steps.

Jane said, "A house has a roof.
Will you put a roof on the house?
How will you make the roof?"

I will make the roof from the lid of the box.

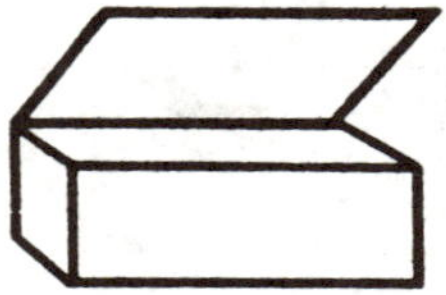

No. There is not enough wood in the lid.

How long is the lid?

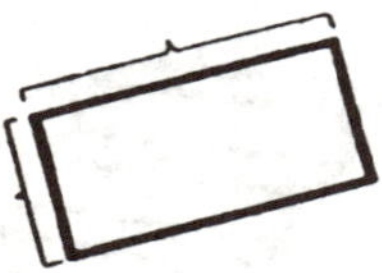

How wide is the lid?

I am measuring it.

The lid is not long enough.
It is not wide enough.

The roof is like this.

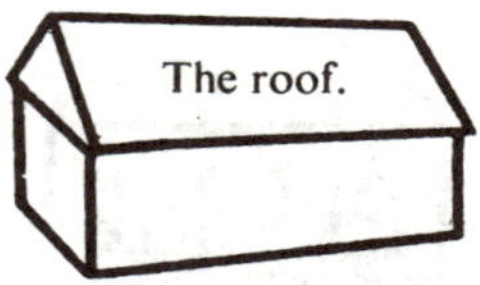

roof [ru:f]
enough [i'nʌf]

wood [wud]
wide [waid]

Here is a wider bit of wood.

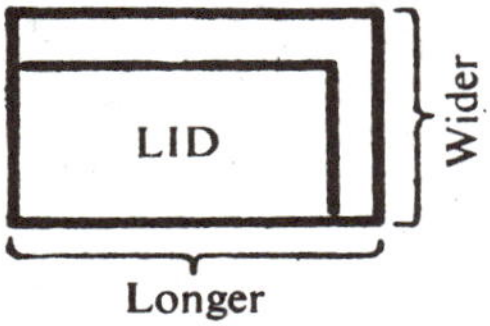

It is wider and it is longer.

I will make the roof from this other bit of wood.

I will make a cut in this wood.

I will make a cut at this angle.

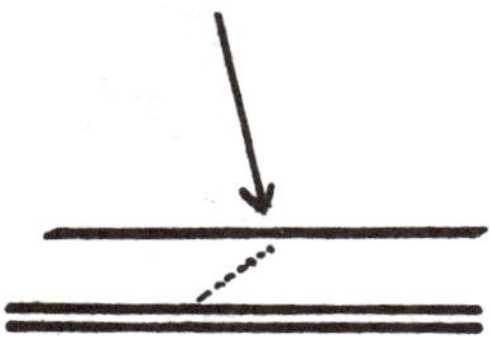

A cut.

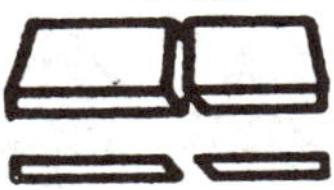

This is an angle.

This is an angle.

wider ['waidə*]
longer ['ləŋgə*]

angle ['æŋgl]

"What are you doing, Tom?"
"I am measuring the wood."

This is a rule.

It is good wood.

This is a tree.

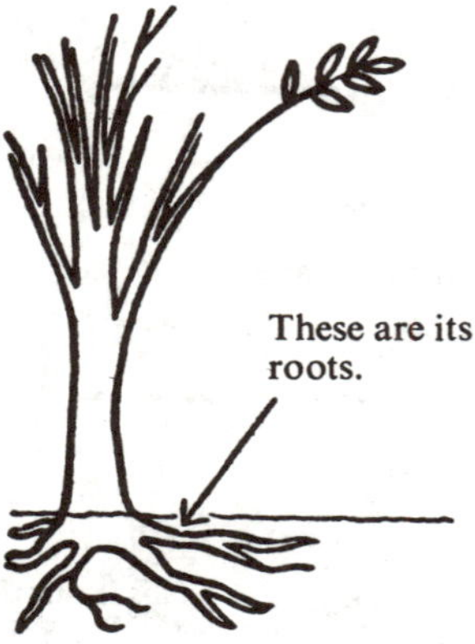

We get wood from trees.

These are trees.

Some wood is hard.
Some wood is soft.

We get hard wood
from some trees.

They give hard wood
to us.

Other trees give soft wood to us.

Now I am making a cut at this angle in this bit of wood.

The blade is going through the wood.

This is my knife.

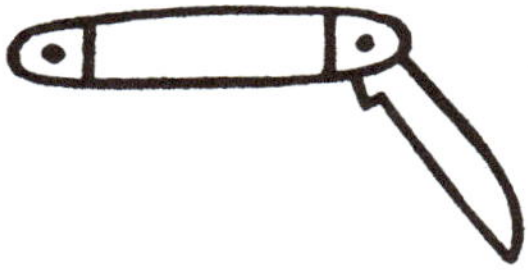

This is the blade of my knife.

I am making a line on the wood.
I am making a line with a pencil.

This is the pencil.

This is the line.

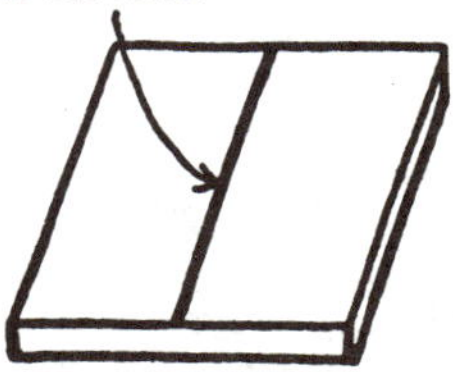

blade [bleid]

pencil ['pensl]

"Keep on the line when you are cutting. Don't go off it."

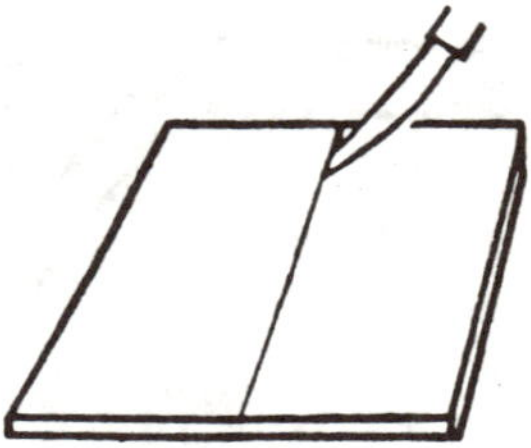

That is bad! The cut is off the line.

cutting [ˈkʌtiŋ]

It's not very bad.

Here is the line.

And here is the cut.

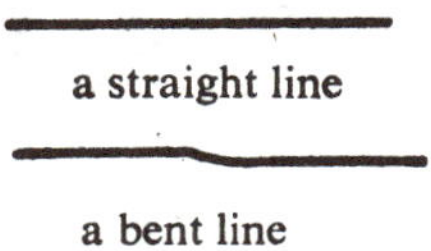

straight [streit]
bent [bent]

Tom is making another attempt.

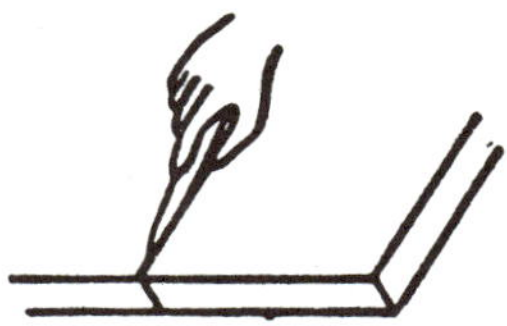

That is better. The cut is straight. The blade of the knife went straight. Good!

attempt [əˈtem*p*t]
better [ˈbetə*]

Now I have these two bits of wood.

I will put them together like this.

There is the roof of the house.

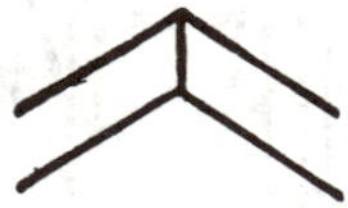

Now I will put the two parts of the roof together with nails.

These are nails.

nails [neilz]

I will make a hole through this part of the roof into the other part of the roof.

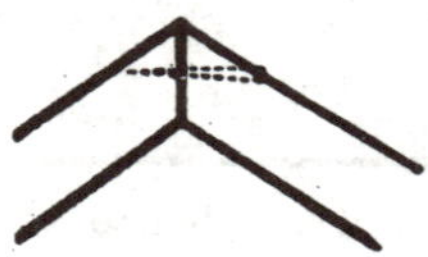

Tom is making the holes for the nails.

Now he is putting the nails in with his hammer.

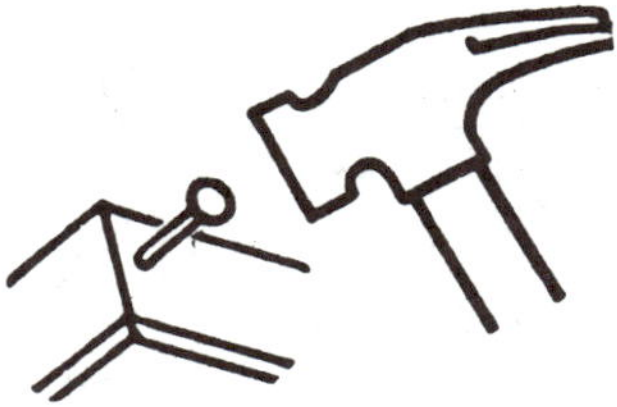

Now the two parts of the roof are together.

The roof is ready.

hammer [ˈhæmə*]

strong [strɔŋ]

Is this line long?

This line is longer.

Is this bit of wood strong?

This bit of wood is stronger.

don't [dount]
broken ['broukən]

wasn't ['wɔznt]
stronger ['strɔŋgə*]

Here are the supports for the roof.

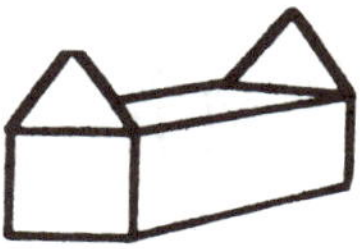

Will you put another support for it in the middle?

Where?

Here.

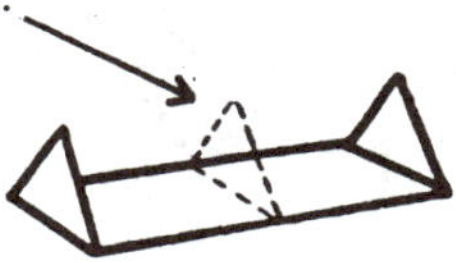

In the middle.

Yes, that is better.

This is a straight line.

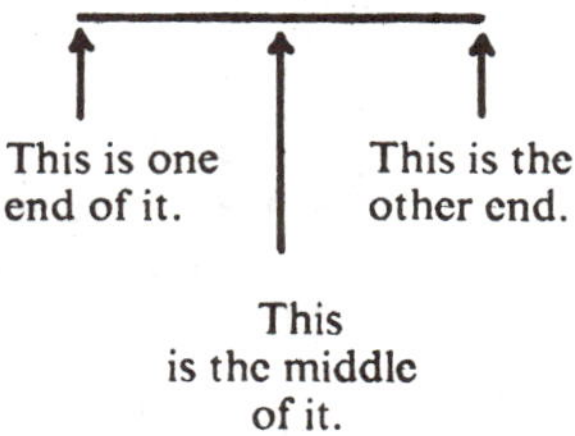

This is a bent line.

That will be better.
That will make the roof stronger.

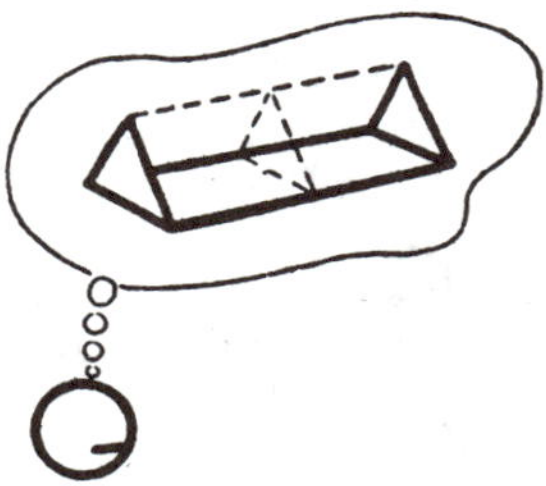

support [sə'pɔ:t]
middle ['midl]

end [end]

Jane is making something.

I am making a coat and trousers.

Here are the trousers.

Here is the coat.

"Has your coat a collar?"

"Yes, it has. Here is the collar."

This is the front of the coat.

Here is the collar of the coat.

This is the back of the coat.

This is one side of it.

This is one pocket of it.

collar [ˈkɔlə*]

Here is the other side.

These are the arms of the coat.

These are the buttons of the coat.

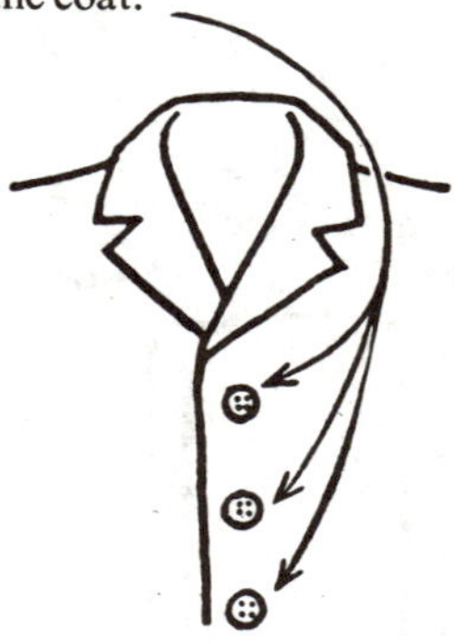

buttons ['bʌtnz]

This is a button.

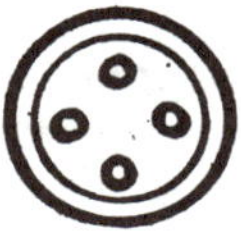

This is a needle.

This is a buttonhole

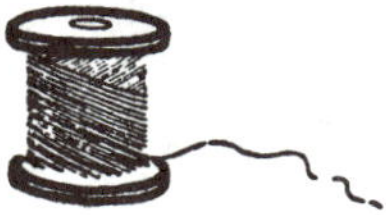

This is thread.

What are you doing with your needle now?

I am putting this button on the coat.

And I am making the buttonholes.

buttonhole [ˈbʌtnhoul]
needle [ˈni:dl]
thread [θred]

The girl will put the end of the thread through the needle.

She has the needle in the fingers of one hand and the thread in the fingers of the other hand.

This is the end of the thread.

This is the hole in the needle.

It is the eye of the needle.

The end of the thread is not going straight. It is not going through the hole in the needle.

The thread did not go through the needle. It is not through the hole in the needle now.

It is on one side of the needle.
It is on this side of the needle.

Now the girl is doing it again.
Is the end of the thread through the hole?
No, it is not. It is on the other side of the needle.

The girl is making another attempt.
This time the thread will go through the hole. The end of the thread is straight.

It went through. The girl is taking the end of the thread in her fingers.
The thread is through the needle.

Where are your scissors?
Here they are.

This blade is narrow. This blade is wide.

Narrow?
This is a narrow street.

This is a wide street.

These trousers are wide. These trousers are narrow

scissors ['sizəz]

narrow ['nærou]

a These are two walls.

Which of them is thicker? Is wall A or wall B thicker?

b These are two cuts.

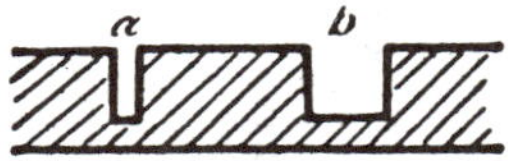

Which of them is wider? Is cut A or cut B wider?

c These are two nails.

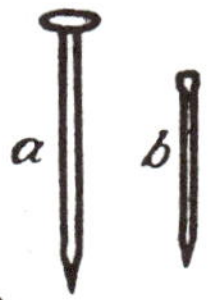

Which of them is longer?

d Which of these two men is stronger?

e Which of these two pencils is shorter?

f Which of these two cards is longer?

Which is wider?

g Which of these three angles is a right angle?

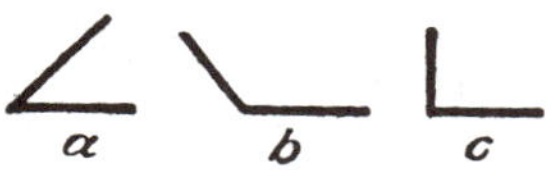

h Which of these things are broken?

Answers are on page 174.

QUESTION

a What is he doing?

b What is she doing?

c What is he doing?

d What is he doing now?

e What is he doing?

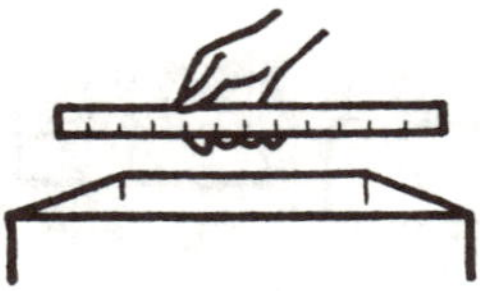

f What is she doing?

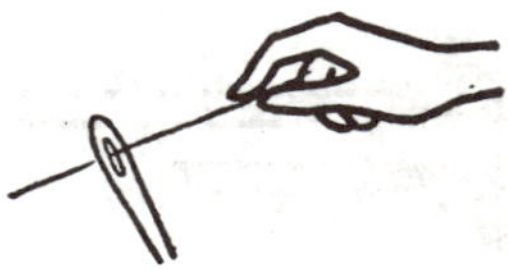

g What is she doing now?

h And what is she doing now?

Answers are on page 174.

A What are these things?

B Which of them go through the air?

C Which of them go on their feet?

D Which of them go on the water?

Answers are on page 174.

Answers to questions on pages 171-173.

Page 171

a Wall B is thicker.

b Cut B is wider.

c Nail A is longer.

d The man who is on his feet is stronger.

e Pencil B is shorter.

f Card B is longer.
Card A is wider.

g Angle C is a right angle.

h The cup, the hammer, and the plate are broken.

Page 172

a He is going up the steps.

b She is going down the steps.

c He is putting a nail in with a hammer.

d He is taking a nail out with a hammer.

e He is measuring a box.

f She is putting a thread through the hole in a needle.

g She is taking the end of the thread between her finger and thumb.

h She is putting a button on with a needle and thread.

Page 173

A

a a train	b its engine	c an aeroplane	d a chair
e a ship	f a flower	g mountains	h trees
i a star	j a cloud	k the sun	l the moon
m a pig	n a sheep	o a horse	p a cow
q a dog	r a goat	s a coat	t a bird
u trousers	v a cup	w a knife	x a spoon
y scissors			

B Aeroplanes and birds go through the air.

C Pigs, sheep, horses, cows, dogs, birds, and goats go on their feet.

D Ships and some birds go on the water.

The earth goes round in twenty-four hours.

There are twenty-four hours in every day.
The sun comes up and goes down every day because the earth is turning round.

The earth goes round the sun in a year.

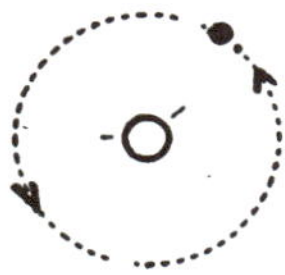

There are three hundred and sixty-five days in a year.
Three hundred and sixty-five days make a year.

There are seven days in a week. Seven days make a week.
Here are the names of the days of the week: Monday, Tuesday, Wednesday, Thursday, Friday, Saturday, Sunday. Monday is before Tuesday. Tuesday is after Monday.

There are thirty-one or thirty or twenty-eight days in a month.
Here are the names of the months:
January (31)
February (28)
March (31)
April (30)
May (31)
June (30)
July (31)
August (31)
September (30)
October (31)
November (30)
December (31).
January is before February...
February is after January...

because [bi'kɔz] · year [jə:*] · month [mʌnθ] · January ['dʒænjuəri] · February ['februəri] · March [mɑ:tʃ] · April ['eiprəl] · June [dʒu:n] · July [dʒu'lai] · August ['ɔ:gəst] · September [sep'təmbə*] · October [ɔk'toubə*] · November [nou'vembə*] · December [di'sembə*]

These are the winter months:
December, January, February.
These are the summer months:
June, July, August.
These are the spring months:
March, April, May.
These are the autumn months:
September, October, November.

In the North, the earth is cold in the winter.
The wind is cold.
Snow comes down from the sky.
There are no leaves on the trees.
There is ice over the water.
The days are short.

In the North, the earth and the air are warm in the summer.
There are leaves on the trees.
The days are long.
There is no ice or snow.

In the spring the leaves come out on the trees.
Plants come up out of the earth, and flowers come out on the plants.

winter ['wintə*]
months [mʌnθs]
summer ['sʌmə*]

spring [spriŋ]
autumn ['ɔ:təm]
snow [snou]

In the autumn, the leaves come down from the branches of the trees.
Autumn is the time of the fall of the leaves.
They are coming down.
They are falling.

In the spring the days get longer.
Every day is longer than the day before it.
In the spring today is longer than yesterday.
In the autumn the days get shorter.
Every day is shorter than the day before it.
In the autumn tomorrow will be shorter than today.

This line

is longer than

this line.

The time between three and four is shorter than the time between three and five.

One hour is a shorter time than two hours.

Fifteen minutes make a quarter of an hour.

Thirty minutes make half an hour.

Forty-five minutes make three quarters of an hour.

---

fall [fɔ:l]
are falling [a:ˈfɔ:liŋ]
than [ðæn; ðən]

minutes [ˈminits]
quarter [ˈkwɔ:tə*]
half [hɑ:f]

Which is shorter—a quarter of an hour or half an hour?

Which is shorter—the minute hand or the hour hand of a clock?

This is an inch.

The distance from A to B is one inch.

Half an inch is a shorter distance than an inch.

A quarter of an inch

Three-quarters of an inch

Twelve inches make a foot.

Three feet make a yard.

This is a yard rule.

There are thirty-six inches in a yard.

This is a foot.

How long is it?
It is ten inches long.

These are feet.

They are not twelve inches long.

distance [ˈdistəns]

Seventeen hundred and sixty yards (1760) make a mile.
In half a mile there are eight hundred and eighty yards.
Miles, yards, feet, and inches are measures of distance.

What are this man and this girl doing?
They are taking a walk.

In one hour he will go two miles, and she will go four miles.
He is slow. She is quick.
She is quicker than he is.
He is slower than she is.

This is a train.

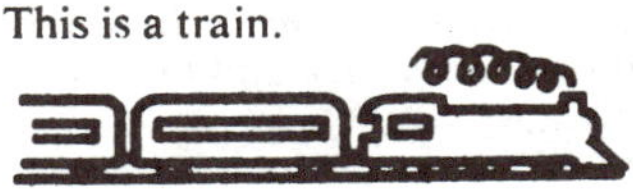

Trains are quicker than horses or men.

This is an aeroplane.

Aeroplanes are quicker than trains or horses or men.

mile [mail]
measure [ˈmeʒə*]
walk [wɔ:k]
slow [slou]

quick [kwik]
quicker [ˈkwikə*]
slower [ˈslouə*]

This baby is one year old.

This boy is ten years old.

This man is thirty years old.

This old man is ninety years old.
That is a stick in his hand.

The baby is very young.
How old is he? He is one year old.
The old man is very old.
How old is he? He is ninety years old.

This box is four inches long and three inches wide and two inches high.

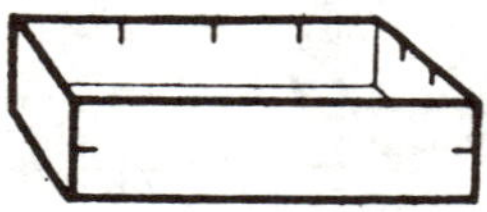

How long is it?
It is four inches long.

This room is twenty feet long and sixteen feet wide and twelve feet high.

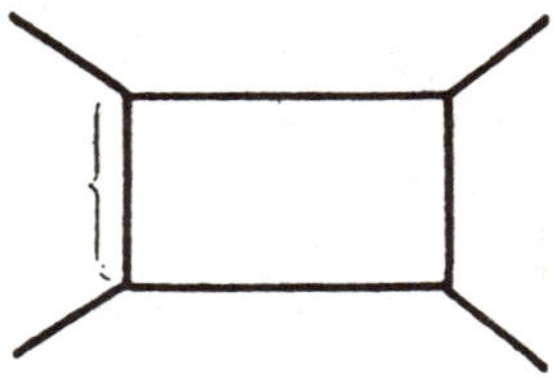

How high is the room? It is twelve feet high.

---

stick [stik]

young [jʌŋ]

This is a short coat.

This is a longer coat.

This is the longest coat of the three.

This is a thin book.

This is a thicker book.

This is the thickest book of the three.

This is a narrow street.

This is a wider street.

This is the widest street of the three.

Which is the narrowest street of the three?

This is a dirty face.

This is a cleaner face.

This is the cleanest face of the three.

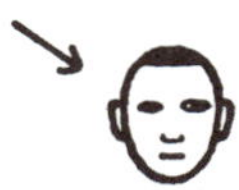

Which is the dirtiest face?

the longest [ðə'lɔŋgist]
the thickest [ðə'θikist]
the widest [ðə'waidist]
the narrowest [ðə'nærou*ist]

cleaner [kli:nə*]
the cleanest [ðə'kli:nist]
the dirtiest [ðə'də:tiist]

Glass
is harder than
wood.

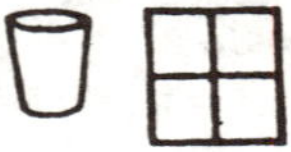

Wood is harder than bread.

Bread is harder than butter.

Which is the softest of these?
Which is the hardest?

This man
is stronger
than this boy.

The boy
is not as
strong as
the man.

He is not as old as the man.

The baby is not as old as the boy
or as strong as the boy.

the softest [ðəˈsɔftist]
the hardest [ðəˈhɑ:dist]
older [ˈouldə*]
the oldest [ðiˈouldist]

This man is
older than this boy.

The boy is
older than
this baby.

Which of
them is the
oldest?
The baby is the
youngest. He is very young.

This line

is as long as this line.

The two lines are equal (=).

This line

is not as long as

this line.

They are not equal.

the youngest [ðəˈjʌŋgist]
as ... as ... [əz ... əz ...]
equal [ˈi:kwəl]

A train may go eighty (80) miles in an hour.

An aeroplane may go three hundred (300) miles in an hour.

Trains and aeroplanes are different sorts (see page 106) of transport.

What are some other sorts of transport?

Ships are another sort of transport.
How far may a quick ship go in an hour?
A quick ship may go thirty miles in an hour.

Cars and horses and carriages are other sorts of transport.

Aeroplanes, trains, ships, cars, and horses and carriages take us from one place to another.

may [mei]
transport [ˈtrænspɔ:t]
far [fɑ:*]

car [kɑ:*]
carriage [ˈkæridʒ]
place [pleis]

We may go on our feet from one place to another.

When we go on our feet, we are walking.

Or we may go in a train or in a ship or in a car or in an aeroplane or on a horse or in a carriage with a horse before it.

Some places are near to one another.

Some places are far from one another.

Places in Washington are near to one another.
The distance from one place to another is not far.
But some places in the United States are far from one another.
Which are nearer to one another?
Which are farther from one another?

are walking [ɑ:ˈwɔ:kiŋ]
near [niə*]

nearer [ˈniərə*]
farther [ˈfɑ:ðə*]

This is a map of North America.

These are mountains.

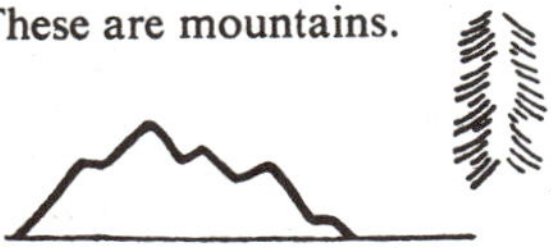

Men go up mountains.
Mountains are high.

These are railways.

These are roads.

These are rivers.

Trains go on railways.

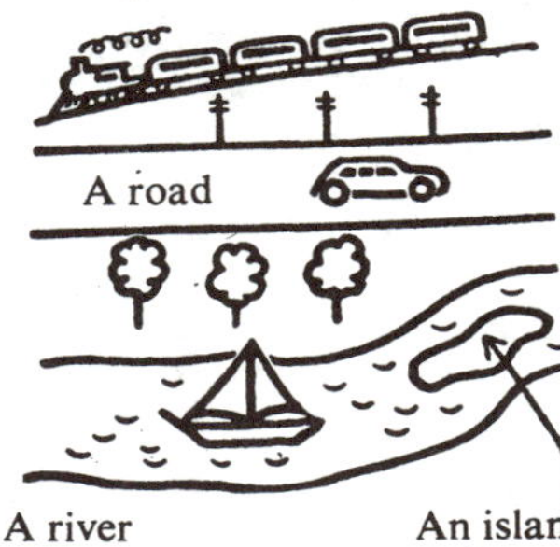

map [mæp] · Mackenzie River [mə'kenzi 'rivə*] · Ottawa ['ɔtəwə] · New York ['nju:'jɔ:k] · Washington ['wɔʃiŋtən] · Mississippi River [misi'sipi 'rivə*] · Mexico City ['meksikou 'siti] · road [roud] · river ['rivə*] · island ['ailənd]

Ottawa, Washington, Mexico City, New York, and Los Angeles are towns.

This is a town.

The government of Canada is in Ottawa.

The government of the United States is in Washington.

The government of Mexico is in Mexico City.

How far is Ottawa from Mexico City?
The distance from Ottawa to Mexico City is about twenty-three hundred miles.
How far is New York from Los Angeles?
The distance between New York and Los Angeles is about twenty-five hundred miles.

How far is the mouth of the Mackenzie River from the mouth of the Mississippi?
The distance is about 3300 miles.
The mouth of a river is the place where it goes into the sea.

government [ˈgʌvnmənt]
Canada [ˈkænədə]

about [əˈbaut]
sea [siː]

This is the earth. We are seeing it from the north.

There is more land than water on this side of the earth.

This is the earth. We are seeing it from the south.

There is more water than land on this side.

This is the moon.

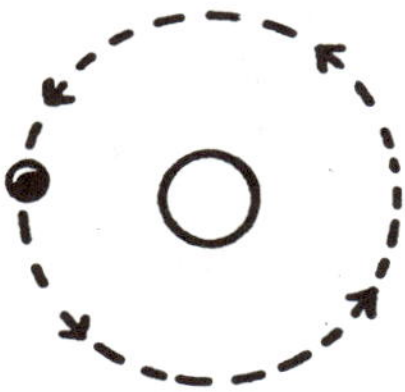

The moon goes round the earth in a month.

Do we ever see the other side of the moon? No.

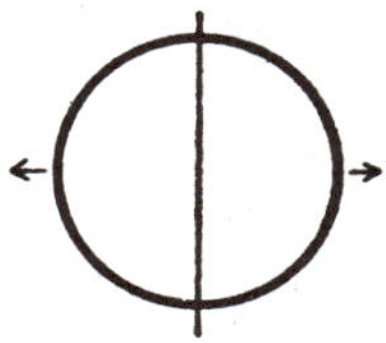

We see the same side of the moon at all times. Why?

more [mɔ:*]
land [lænd]

why [wai]

We see the same side at all times because the moon is turning round.

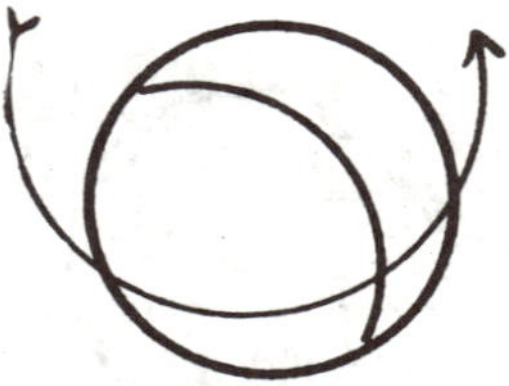

It is going round the earth and it is turning round itself.
It keeps the same side to the earth.

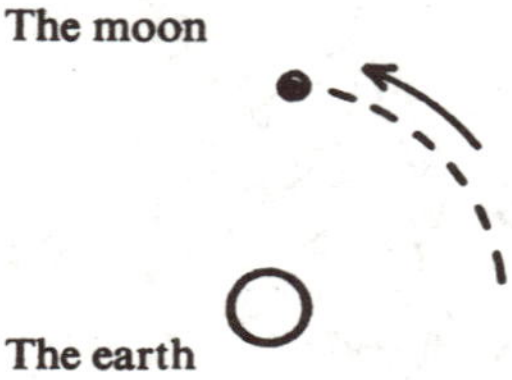

We see the same side of the moon at all times.
Sometimes we see it like this.

One half of the moon is dark.

The other half is bright.

This is a half moon.

Sometimes we see the moon like this.

This part of the moon is dark.

This part of it is bright.

This is a quarter moon.

is turning [iz'tə:niŋ]
itself [it'self]
sometimes ['sʌmtaimz]

dark [dɑ:k]
bright [brait]

Sometimes we see it like this.
This is a new moon.

This is a new hat.

This is an old hat.

And sometimes we see it like this.
This is a full moon.

This glass is full.

This glass is not full.

These are the changes of the moon.

Full,
three-quarters,
half,
a quarter,
new.

But at all times we see the same side of the moon.

Change? What is that?

Here is a change in the direction of this line.

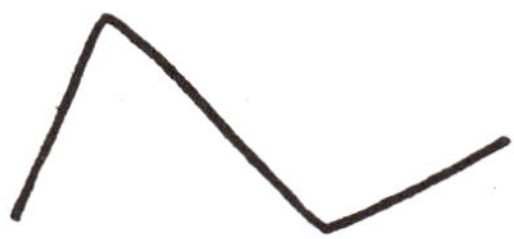

And here is another change.

full [ful]

change [tʃeindʒ]

Here are two trains.
The man was in this train.
He is going to the other train.
He is making a change.
He is changing trains.

The potatoes were hard. After a time they were soft. There was a change in the potatoes.

This water was cold.

Now it is boiling.
That is a change.

There was a change in the water.

In the summer the leaves are on the trees.

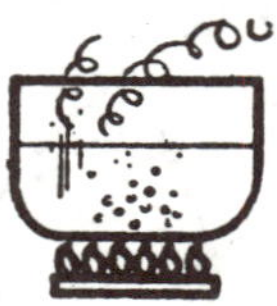

In the autumn the leaves fall off the trees.
That is a change.

is changing [iz'tʃeindʒiŋ]

I took a newspaper and gave a dollar ($ 1) to the man.

He took the dollar and he gave

a half dollar 

and a quarter (dollar) 

and twenty cents 

This is the money which he gave to me with the paper.

The price of the paper was five cents. I got the paper and ninety-five cents from him.

$ 1.00 —	100 cents
Paper —	5 cents
	95 cents

That money was my change.
I had a dollar.
After I got the paper I had the paper and ninety-five cents. I did not have the dollar.
That was a change.

cent [sent]

price [prais]

a Is the boy nearer to the woman than the girl is?

Is the girl nearer to the boy than to the woman?

b Which of these two is farther from the tree?

Is the boy farther from the tree than from the girl?

c Which of these two glasses is full of water, the glass on the right or the glass on the left?

d Is there more land than water on the south side of the earth?

Answers are on page 194.

a Which of these is a half moon, which is a full moon, which is a quarter moon, and which is a new moon?

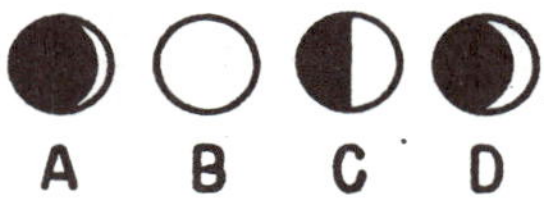

b I got a book. I gave three dollars to the man in the bookshop.
He gave me the book and fifty cents. What was the price of the book? How much was the book? How much change did he give me?

c How far may a quick train go in an hour? How far may you go on your feet in an hour, four miles or forty?

d What are some different sorts of transport? Which is the quickest sort of transport?

bookshop [ˈbukʃɔp]
quickest [ˈkwikist]

Answers are on page 194.

Answers to questions on pages 192-193.

Page 192

a No, the girl is nearer to the woman. Yes, the girl is nearer to the boy than to the woman.

b The girl is farther from the tree. Yes, the boy is farther from the tree than from the girl.

c The glass to the left is full of water.

d No. There is more water than land on the south side of the earth.

Page 193

a C is a half moon;
B is a full moon;
D is a quarter moon;
and A is a new moon.

b The price of the book was \$ 2.50. It was \$ 2.50. He gave me 50 cents change.

c A quick train may go a hundred miles in an hour. I may go four miles but not forty.

d Ships, trains, horses and carriages, and aeroplanes are different sorts of transport. The aeroplane is the quickest of these.

The distance through the earth from North to South is seven thousand nine hundred (7900) miles.

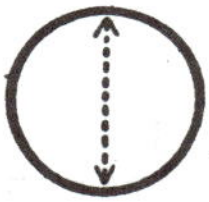

The distance round the earth is twenty-four thousand nine hundred (24,900) miles.

What is that in your hand?
It is a ball.
The ball is small.

What is that in the sky?
It is the sun.
The sun is great.
The sun is a great ball of fire.

ball [bɔ:l]
small [smɔ:l]

How far is the moon from the earth?
It is two hundred and forty thousand (240,000) miles from the earth.

How far is the sun from the earth?
The distance of the sun from the earth is ninety-three million (93,000,000) miles.

What is the size of the sun?
It is 864,000 miles through from one side to the other.

fire [ˈfaiə*]
size [saiz]

What is the size of the moon?
It is two thousand one hundred and sixty (2160) miles through from one side to the other.
Is the moon smaller than the earth?
Is the earth smaller than the sun?
Is the sun greater than the moon?

The moon is near the earth. The earth is far from the sun.
New York is near Washington.
San Francisco is far from Washington.

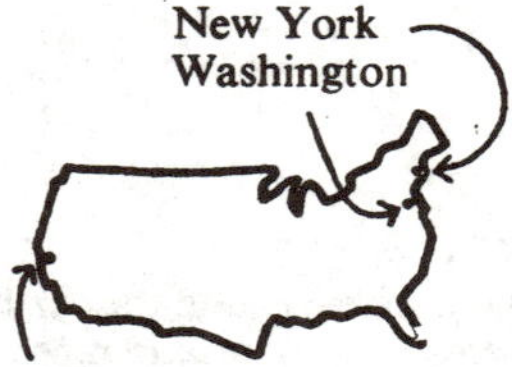

Are the stars smaller than the sun?
No. Some of the stars are much greater than the sun.
Are they nearer than the sun?
No, they are much farther than the sun.

How far from the earth is the nearest star?
It is over four light-years from the earth.
What is a light-year?
It is the distance which light goes in a year.

smaller ['smɔ:lə*]
greater ['greitə*]

the nearest [ðə'niərist]
light-year ['lait-jə:*]

This is a flame.
It sends out light.

The sun sends out light.
The light goes out from the sun in every direction.

Light goes 186,300 miles in a second.
How far does it go in a year?

It goes about
6,000,000,000,000
miles in a year.

A light-year is
6,000,000,000,000
miles.

The nearest star is over four light-years from the earth.

The nearest star is
25,000,000,000,000
miles from
the earth.
The nearest stars are very far from us.
Some of the stars are very much farther.
The farthest stars are thousands of light-years from us.

second ['sekənd]

the farthest [ðə'fɑ:ðist]

The sun sends its light out in every direction.

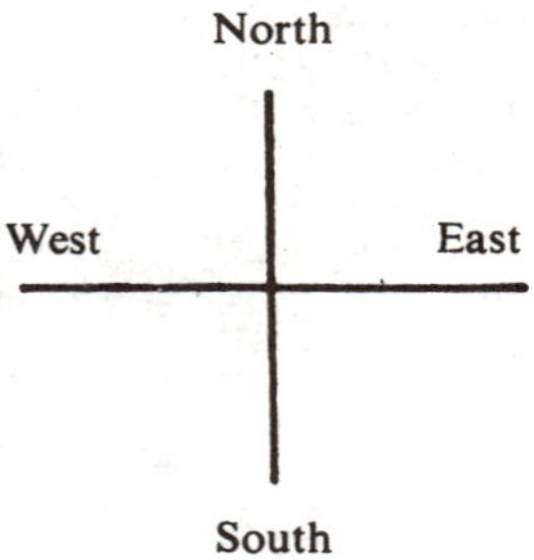

These are four directions.

Up and down are two other directions.

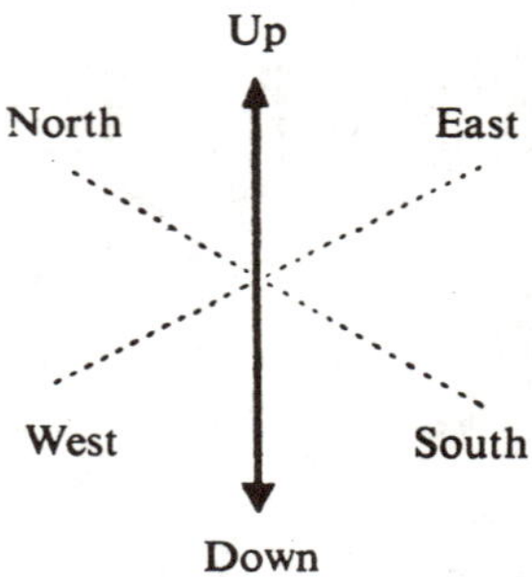

This boy has six apples in his hands.
He is on a branch of a tree.

He will send the six apples in different directions.

He sent one apple north, another apple south, another east, and another west.

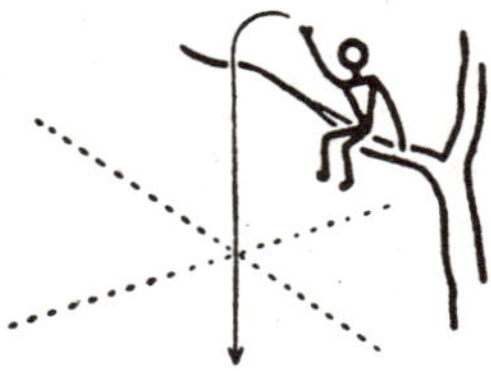

He sent another apple down.
He sent five apples in five directions.

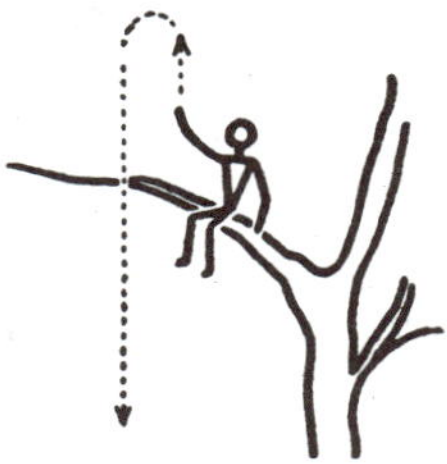

He sent the last apple up. But then it came down.
Why did it come down?

The first apple went north and then it came down. The other apples went south and east and west and then they all came down to the earth.

They all came down to the earth?
Why did they come down?

The first apple...
The last apple...
What is "the first"...?
What is "the last"...?

These men are in a line.
This is the first man.

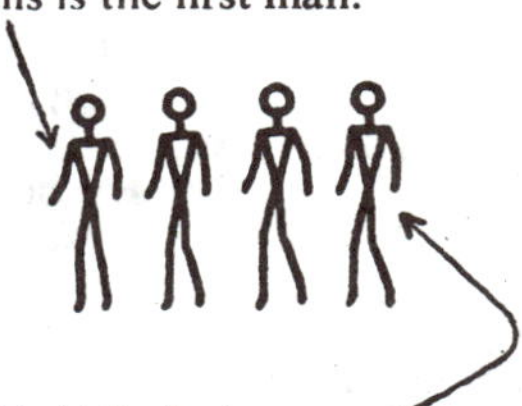

This is the last man.

Here are three dogs.
Which is the first dog?
Which is the last dog?
The other dog is the dog in the middle.
He is between the first dog and the last dog.
Two of the dogs are white.
The other dog is black.
The dog in the middle is black.

last [lɑ:st]
first [fə:st]

black [blæk]

Here are two bodies.
One is a great body.
It is the earth.
The other is a small body. It is an apple.
The apple is coming down to the earth. Why?

It is coming down because there is an attraction between the two bodies.
The attraction between them makes the apple come down.

All bodies which have weight have an attraction for one another.

Here are two bodies.
These are springs.

Which body has the greater weight?

Here are two men.

This man is thin.	This man is fat.
His body is thin.	His body is fat.

Which man's weight is greater?

bodies [ˈbɔdiz]
attraction [əˈtrækʃən]

weight [weit]
fat [fæt]

This is a scale.

A scale is an instrument for measuring weight.

Which man's weight is greater? They are on the scale.

The weight of the thin man is 100 pounds.

The weight of the fat man is 200 pounds.

Clocks are instruments for measuring time.

This is a watch.

Watches and clocks are instruments for measuring time.

This is an instrument for measuring heat.

A yard rule is an instrument for measuring distance.

Inches, feet, yards, metres, and miles are measures of distance.

scale [skeil]
pound [paund]
watch [wɔtʃ]

watches [ˈwɔtʃiz]
metre [ˈmi:tə*]

All bodies have an attraction for one another.

If the bodies are great the attraction between them is great.

If the bodies are small the attraction is small.

If the bodies go farther from one another the attraction gets smaller.

Distance	Attraction
1	1
2	1/4
3	1/9
4	1/16
5	1/25

Here is a light.

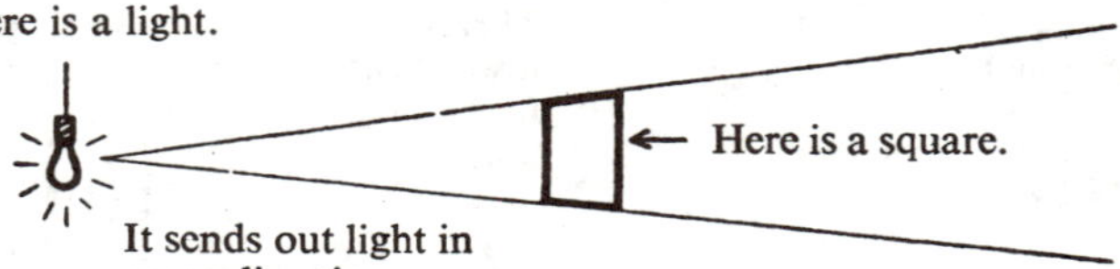

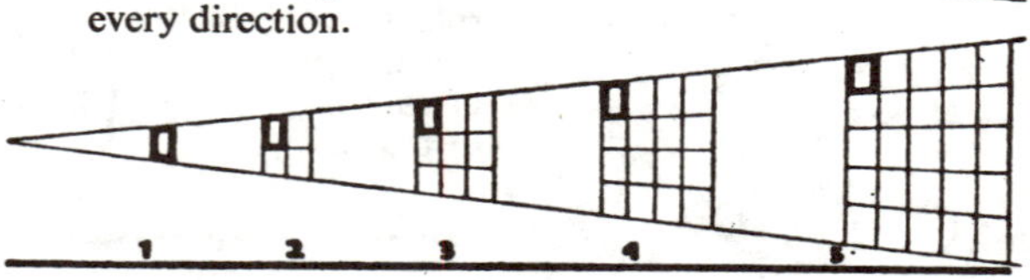

I put the square at different distances from the light. At distance 1, it gets all the light which is going out between the lines. At distance 2, it gets one-fourth of the light. At distance 5, it gets one twenty-fifth. It is the same with the attraction between bodies.

if [if]
square [skwɛə*]
fourth [fɔ:θ]
twenty-fifth [ˈtwenti-ˈfifθ]

What keeps the moon up in the sky?
Why does not the moon come down?

The moon is a great body. Its weight is great.
The earth is a great body. Its weight is eighty-one times the weight of the moon.
Two times three is six.
$2 \times 3 = 6$

The moon and the earth are not very far from one another.
The distance between them is about two hundred and thirty-nine thousand (239,000) miles.

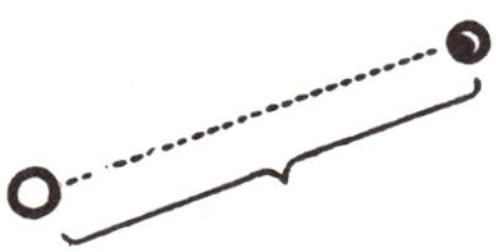

Because they are great bodies and near one another, the attraction between the moon and the earth is very great.
Why does the moon not come down to the earth?
That is a question.

The answer is: "Because it is going round the earth."

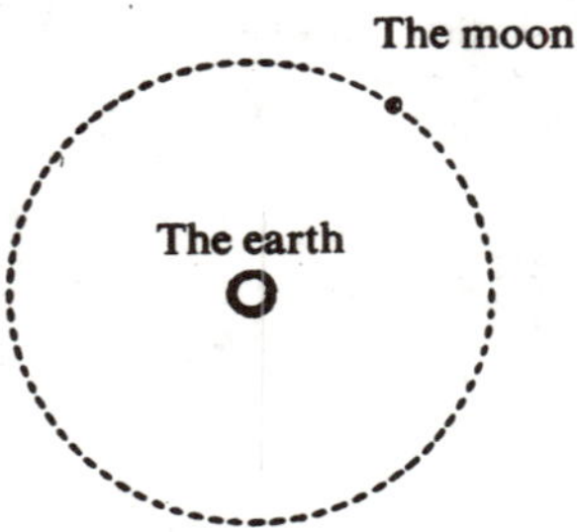

This is a cord in my hand. The cord has a weight at its end.

The weight is hanging down on the cord which is in my hand.

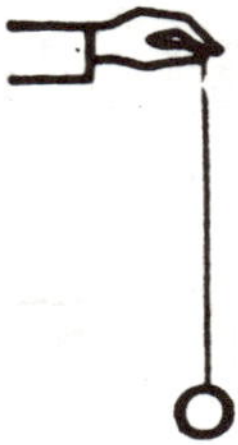

I make the weight go round on the cord.

I keep the end of the cord in my hand.

Now I let the end of the cord in my hand go.

The weight goes off in a straight line. It takes the cord with it.

is hanging [iz ˈhæŋiŋ]

The pull of the cord in my hand kept the weight from going off in a straight line.

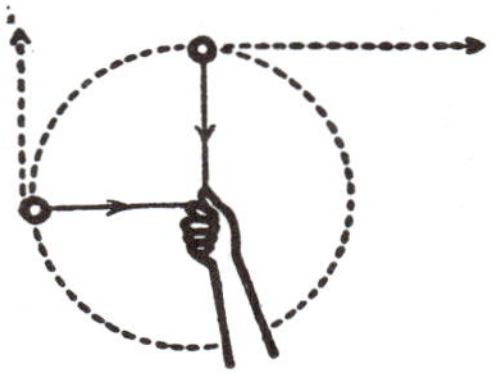

The attraction between the earth and the moon keeps the moon from going off in a straight line.

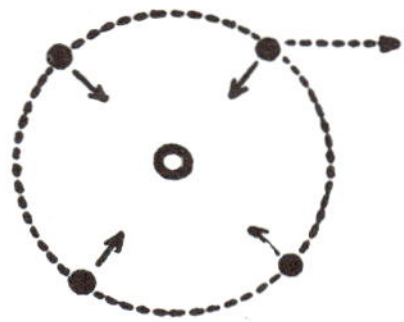

The moon goes round and round the earth... month after month.

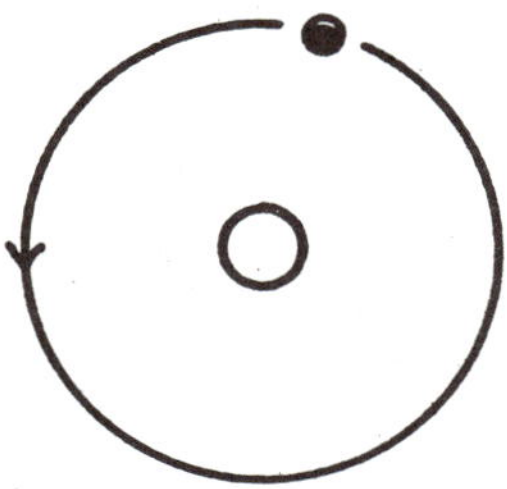

It does not get farther from the earth

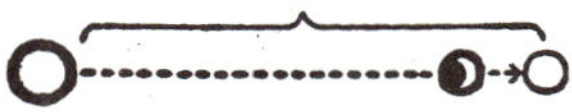

or nearer to the earth.

It keeps about the same distance from the earth.

pull [pul]

kept [kept]

Here is Sir Isaac Newton, the great man of science. Newton had a great mind.

He is under an apple tree.

It is the year 1666.

Those are apples which are over his head.

The seat has three legs.

Here is an apple which was over his head.
The apple was on a branch of the tree.

The apple came off the branch.
It came down.

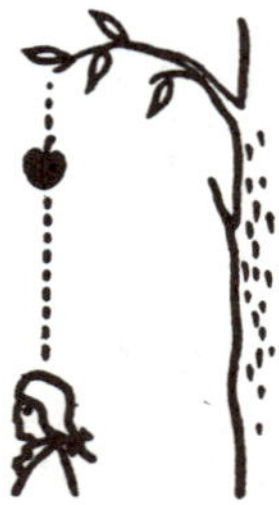

It came down on Newton's head.

Sir Isaac Newton [sə:rˈaizək ˈnju:tn]
science [ˈsaiəns]

mind [maind]
1666 [ˈsiksˈti:nˈsikstiˈsiks]

That is the story.
The story may be true or it may not be true.

But that is the story.
It comes from the great writer, Voltaire.

True?
2 + 2 = 4. That is true.
2 + 2 = 5. That is not true.
It is a false statement.
"Apples are fruit."
That statement is true.
"Apples are animals."
That statement is false.
False = not true
Short = not long
Shut = not open

In this story the fall of the apple on Newton's head was the cause of the idea.

The blow which the apple gave to Newton's head gave an idea to Newton. It made a question come into Newton's mind.

This was the question: "Have the fall of the apple and the motion of the moon the same cause?"

true [tru:]
writer ['raitə*]
false [fɔ:ls]
statement ['steitmənt]

cause [kɔ:z]
idea [ai'diə]
blow [blou]
motion ['mouʃən]

Here is a ball. It is hanging on a cord.

I will give a blow to the ball with this stick.

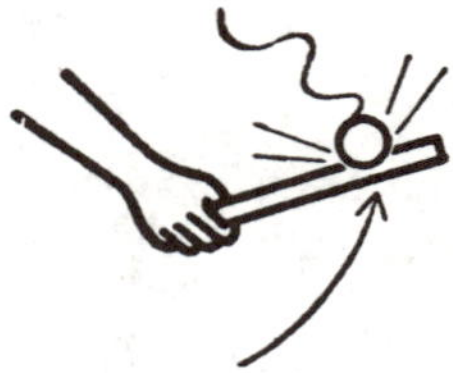

I gave the blow.
Now the ball is in motion.
What was the cause of the motion?
The blow of the stick was the cause of the motion.

The ball was not in motion before the blow.
It was at rest. It was hanging on the end of the cord.

The blow was the cause of the motion.

After the blow the ball was in motion.
The motion came from the blow.
The motion was the effect of the blow.

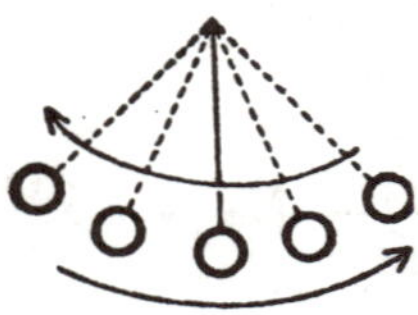

rest [rest]

effect [i'fekt]

QUESTIONS

Which of the statements on this page are true and which are false? Put a T before the true statements and an F before the false.

a 1. The earth is in motion.
  2. The earth is turning round.
  3. The earth goes round the moon.

b 1. The moon is greater than the sun.
  2. The sun is colder than the moon.
  3. The moon goes round the earth.

c 1. The attraction between two bodies gets greater as they go farther from one another.
  2. The attraction between two bodies is greater when they are nearer.
  3. When two great bodies are near one another the attraction between them is small

d 1. When a blow puts a ball in motion, the blow is the cause of the motion.
  2. When a blow puts a ball in motion, the motion is the effect of the blow.
  3. When a body is in motion it is at rest.

Answers are on page 212.

Milk comes from a cow. Heat comes from the sun, or a fire. Where do these things come from?

a potatoes	b cheese	c light
d letters	e flowers	f snow
g oranges	h meat	i eggs

Which of these things have a face?

a man	a dog	a bone	a refrigerator
a clock	a tree	a goat	a bird
an aeroplane	a river	a table	

Which of them have a mouth?
Which of them have hands?
Which of them have a door?

Answers are on page 212.

a We put a bottle on a shelf. Which of these things may we put on a shelf: a book, a mountain, a cup, a box, a star, a clock, a horse, a distance, a plate, a carriage, a river, a house, a spoon, a garden?

b We put potatoes in a saucepan. Which of these things may we put in a saucepan: water, windows, food, streets, tables, milk, soup, trains, salt, colours, eggs, wood, ideas?

c We put money in our pockets. Which of these things may we put in our pockets: pipes, education, letters, pencils, offices, islands, maps, hands, governments, buttons, watches, distance, balls, roofs, knives?

d We put our hats on. Which of these things may we put on: feet, boots, chairs, gloves, shirts, walls, directions, coats, buildings, soap, scissors, collars, locks, socks, trousers, branches, trays, shoes, apples?

Answers are on page 212.

Answers to questions on pages 209-211.

Page 209

a 1. T	b 1. F	c 1. F
2. T	2. F	2. T
3. F	3. T	3. F
d 1. T		
2. T		
3. F		

Page 210

a from the roots of a plant	b from milk	c from the sun or flames
d from persons	e from plants or from seeds	f from the sky or clouds
g from orange trees	h from animals	i from birds

A man, a dog, a clock, a goat, a bird may have a face.
A man, a dog, a goat, a bird, a river may have a mouth.
A man and a clock may have hands.
A refrigerator and an aeroplane may have a door.

Page 211

a a book, a cup, a box, a clock, a plate, a spoon.
b water, food, milk, soup, salt, eggs.
c pipes, letters, pencils, maps, hands, buttons, watches, balls, knives.
d boots, gloves, shirts, coats, collars, socks, trousers, shoes.

What is this?
The man has an umbrella in his hand.
It is open.
He has it over his head. Why?

Because it is raining.
Water is coming down from the sky.
The water is rain.
Rain is coming down.
Rain is falling.
It is raining.

The rain made the man put up his umbrella. That was the effect of the rain.
Today is Monday.
Yesterday (Sunday) the sun was bright.
There were no clouds in the sky.

Today there are dark clouds in the sky.
They come between us and the sun.
The dark clouds keep the light of the sun from us.

umbrella [ʌmˈbrelə]

is raining [izˈreiniŋ]
rain [rein]

The rain comes down from the clouds on me.
It comes down on my head.

The rain comes down from the clouds on us.
It comes down on our heads.

Why is it raining today?
Yesterday the weather was good.
The sun was bright.
The air was warm.

weather [ˈweðə*]

Today the weather is bad. The rain is coming down. The wind is blowing. It is cold and the rain makes us wet.

is blowing [izˈblouiŋ]

Tomorrow the weather may be worse.
It may be very cold. All the water may be ice.
Snow may be coming down making everything white.
Will tomorrow be like this?
Is this winter or summer?

Or tomorrow the weather may be better.
The sun may be bright again. The air may be warm again and the streets may be dry again.
Will tomorrow be like this?

worse [wə:s]

everything [ˈevriθiŋ]

What are the causes of these changes in the weather? Change? What is that? (See page 190.)

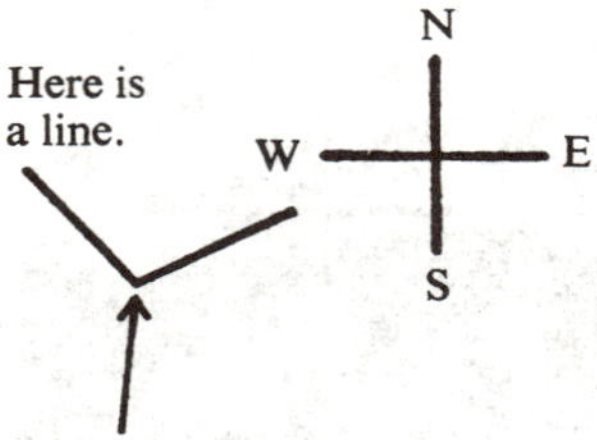

Here is a change in the direction of the line.

This bird was wet. It was in the rain.

Now it is dry.

That is a change. It was wet. It is dry.

What is the cause of these changes in the weather?

Good	Bad
Dry	Wet
Warm	Cold

Weather

Why are there these changes of weather?

There is not one cause only. There are numbers of causes. Changes in the heat which comes to us from the sun are one cause of changes of weather.

only ['ounli]

The amount of heat which the earth gets from the sun is different from time to time. There are changes in the sun.

If you take a look at the sun through a bit of dark glass you may see small marks on the face of the sun.

Amount? One dollar is a small amount of money. A million dollars is a great amount of money.

A drop of rain is a very small amount of water.

There is a small amount of water in this glass.

There is a great amount of water in the sea.
This is the sea.
Those are ships which are on the sea.

amount [ə'maunt]

mark [mɑ:k]
drop [drɔp]

Changes in the heat which comes to the earth from the sun are one cause of changes in the weather. This discovery is new. A man of science made the discovery in 1944.

He made it by measuring the heat which comes to the earth every day from the sun.
The amount of heat is different from day to day.

On some days the sun sends more heat to the earth. On other days it sends less heat to the earth.

Men are making new discoveries every day. Columbus made the discovery of America in 1492. Columbus went to America in his ship in 1492.

There is more water in this glass than in that.

More Less

discovery [dis'kʌvəri]
less [les]
discoveries [dis'kʌvəriz]

Columbus [kə'lʌmbəs]
1492 ['fɔː'tiːn'naintituː]

What were some other great discoveries?
One of them was fire.

Fire is of very great use to men. It gives us heat.

Another great discovery was the wheel.

Wheels are round.

They go round.

A cart

They are of very great use to man.

Another great discovery were clothes.

What are these?
These are some other sorts of clothes

A skirt

A shirt

The making of cloth was a great discovery.
This is how we make cloth.

These are threads. (See page 167.)
They go across from one side to the other of a frame.

---

smoke [smouk]
use [ju:s]
wheel [wi:l]
cart [kɑ:t]
skirt [skə:t]
across [əˈkrɔs]

These are other threads.

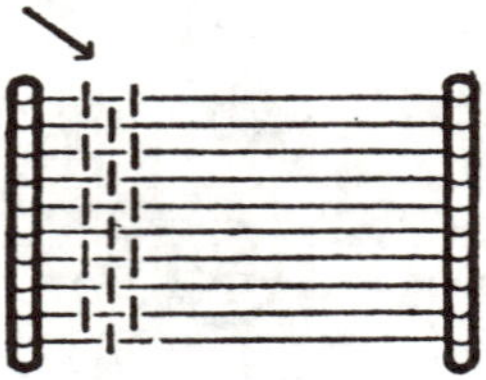

They go across the first threads.

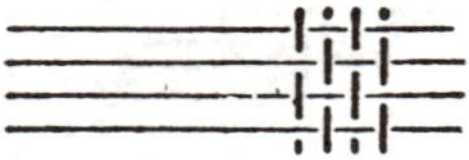

They go under and over them.

This is cloth.

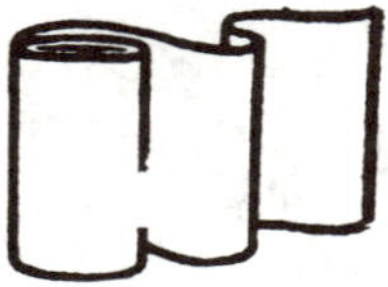

This is a roll of cloth.
We make clothes of cloth. We make cloth of threads.

We make threads from wool and cotton and silk.

We get wool from sheep.

Wool is the thick warm hair of sheep.
Men take the wool off the sheep's back with scissors.

roll [roul]
wool [wul]

cotton [ˈkɔtn]
silk [silk]

We make threads from the wool by twisting the hairs round and round.

That wheel is going round.
It is giving a twist to the thread.
It is twisting the thread.

We get cotton from the cotton plant.

Cotton is the soft white hair round the seeds of the plant.

These are different sorts of seeds.

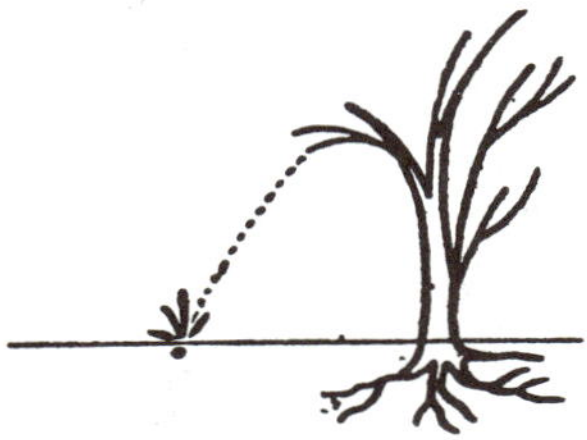

Plants come up from seeds which come from other plants of the same sort.

twisting [ˈtwistiŋ]
twist [twist]
seed [siːd]

We get silk from the silkworm.

This worm makes a soft strong thread of silk and puts it round itself like a coat.

silkworm [ˈsilkwəːm]
worm [wəːm]

Wool, cotton, and silk are different sorts of cloth. We make clothes of all these sorts of cloth. (See page 81.)

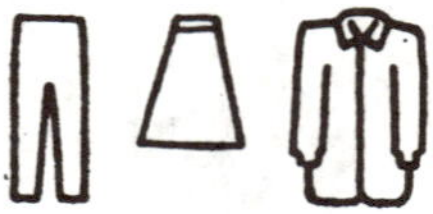

When the weather is cold we put on thick warm wool clothes.
When the weather is warm we put on thin cotton clothes.
Cotton clothes are not as warm as wool clothes.

Thick clothes keep us warm. They keep us warmer than thin clothes.
Thick cloth keeps air in it, between the threads.
The air does not let heat go through it.

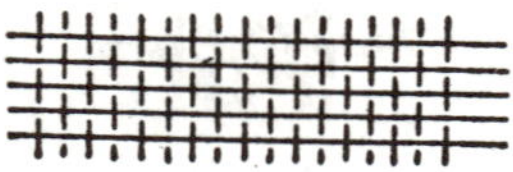

A thick roof keeps the heat of the house in.

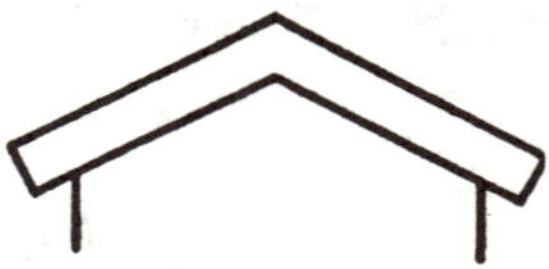

A thin roof lets the heat go through it.

A thick roof keeps the heat of the sun out.

Here is a pencil.
It is straight. It is not bent.

Here is a glass of water.

I put the pencil in the water.

The pencil seems bent where it goes into the water.

The pencil is straight but it seems bent.

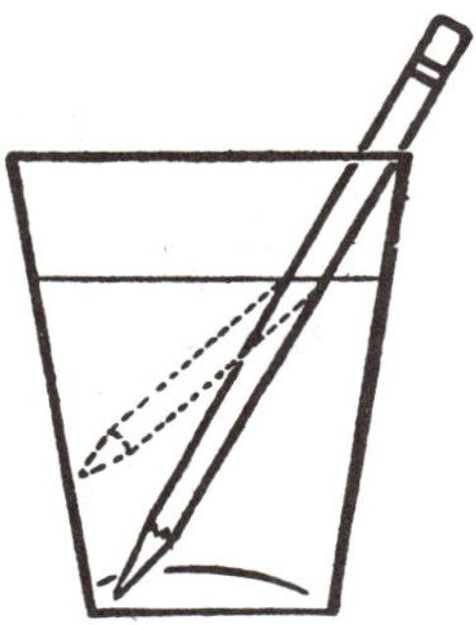

It seems like this.

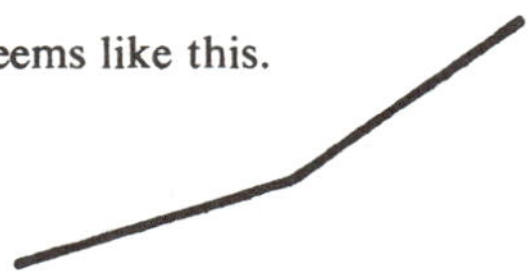

But it is like this.

It is straight, not bent.
It seems bent, not straight.

seems [si:mz]

Before I put the pencil in the water it seemed straight. It was straight.

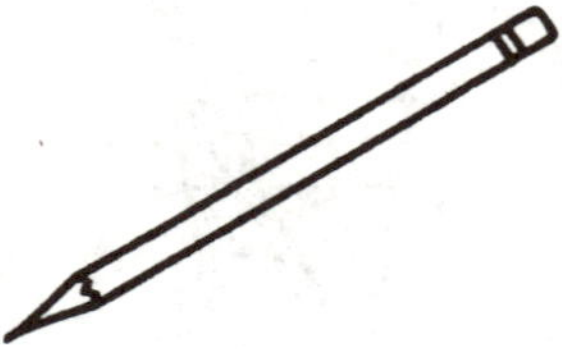

After I put it in the water it seemed bent.
It wasn't bent.

When it is in the water it seems bent.

When it is out of the water we see that it is straight.

Why did it seem bent when it was in the water?

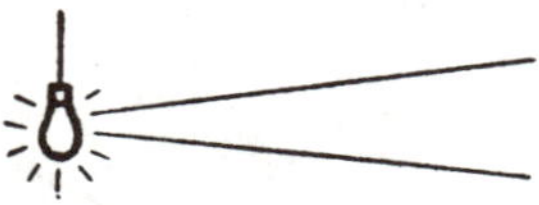

This is a light.
A light sends out light.
The light which it sends out goes in straight lines.

Here is a bit of glass.
A ray of light is going through the glass.

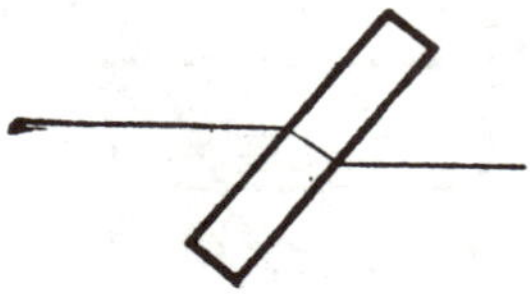

seemed [si:md]

ray [rei]

Where the light goes into the glass, it is bent.

It is bent again where it comes out of the glass into the air.

Here is your eye. 

You are looking at the pencil in the glass of water.

The light from the pencil is bent where it comes out of the water into the air.

It is bent here.

The pencil is not bent.
But the light from it is bent.

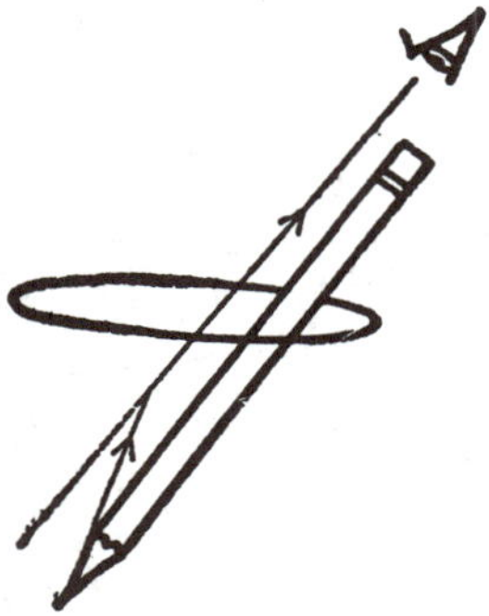

looking [ˈlukiŋ]

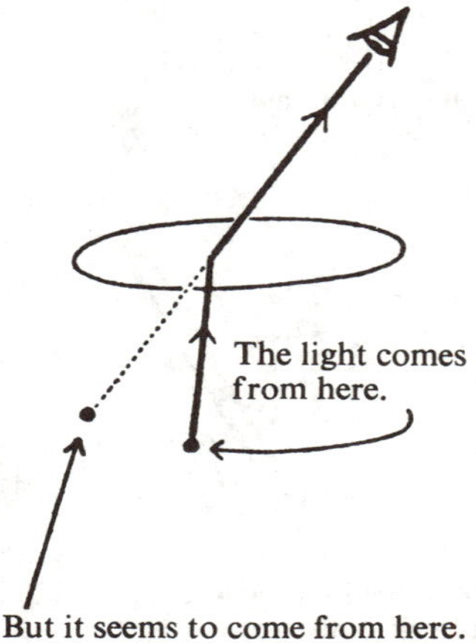

The part of the pencil which is under the water seems to be where it is not.

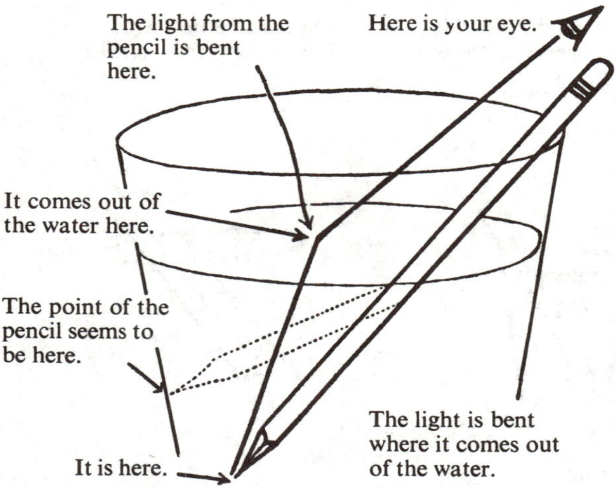

point [pɔint]

This is a looking-glass.

What do you see in the looking-glass?
I see a girl's face in the glass.

She is looking at herself in the glass.
What does she see in the looking-glass?
She sees herself in the glass.

She seems to be here.

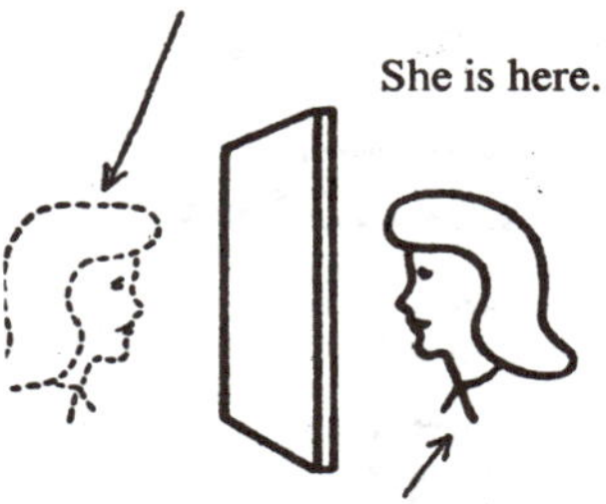

She is on this side of the glass. She seems to be on the other side of the glass.

Why? Because the glass sends the light back.

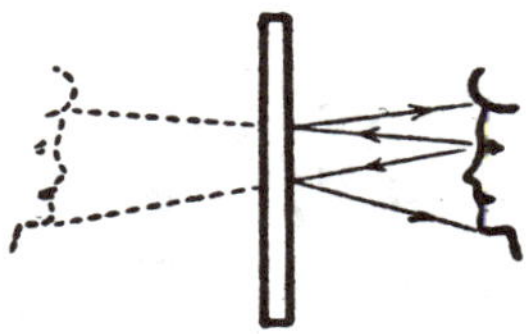

There seem to be two girls in this picture. There is only one.

looking-glass [ˈlukiŋglɑ:s]

herself [hə:ˈself]

What is this man doing?
He is working with a spade. That is his work.

What is this woman doing?
She is working with her needle. That is her work.

What is this man doing?
He is making shoes. He is a shoemaker. That is his work.

These are shoes.

These are boots.

He makes boots and shoes. That is his work.

is working [iz'wə:kiŋ]
spade [speid]

shoemaker ['ʃu:meikə*]
boots [bu:ts]

What is this man doing?
He is putting paint on the door.
He is painting the door. He is a painter. That is his work.

This is his paint.

This is his brush.

He puts the paint on with his paint brush.

This is addition.

The boy is doing addition. That is his work.

This is a bank.

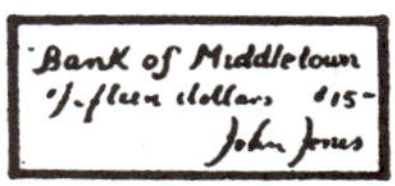

This is a cheque.

paint [peint]
is painting [izˈpeintiŋ]
painter [ˈpeintə*]

addition [əˈdiʃən]
bank [bæŋk]
cheque [tʃek]

We keep money in banks.
Banking is an important sort of business.
Men and women in banks and business houses keep accounts.

This is an account.

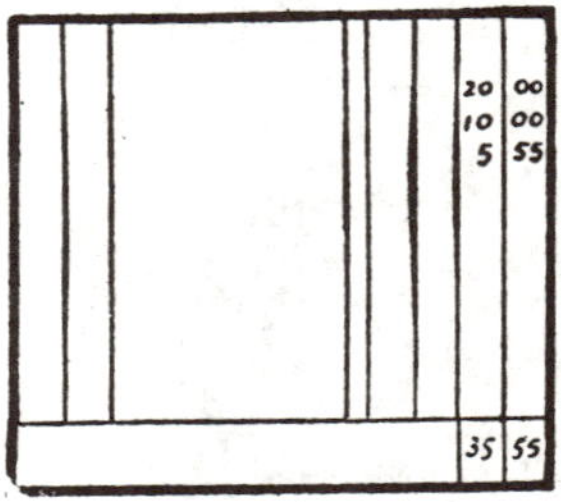

Keeping accounts is an important part of business.

Keeping accounts is one sort of work.

These are account books.

Farming is another sort of work.

This is a farm.

banking ['bæŋkiŋ]
important [im'pɔ:tənt]
business ['biznis]

account [ə'kaunt]
farming ['fɑ:miŋ]
farm [fɑ:m]

This is a cart.

This is a plough.

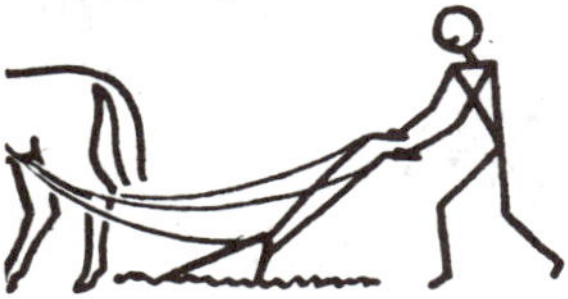

The plough is turning up the earth.

This is a field.

The farmer is ploughing the field. That is part of his work as a farmer.

The farmer has an account with his bank.
He puts his money in the bank.
He keeps money in the bank.
He gets money from the bank.

The account says how much money he has in the bank.
Farming and keeping accounts are two different sorts of work.

plough [plau]
is turning up [iz 'tə:niŋ 'ʌp]
field [fi:ld]

is ploughing [iz'plauiŋ]
farmer ['fɑ:mə*]

What sort of work is this man doing?
He is cutting wood.

What sort of work is this woman doing?
She is washing stockings and dresses.

What sort of work does this man do?
He keeps a shop.

It is a fruit shop.
He is a shopkeeper.

shopkeeper [ˈʃɔpki:pə*]

What sort of work does this woman do?
She keeps a house.

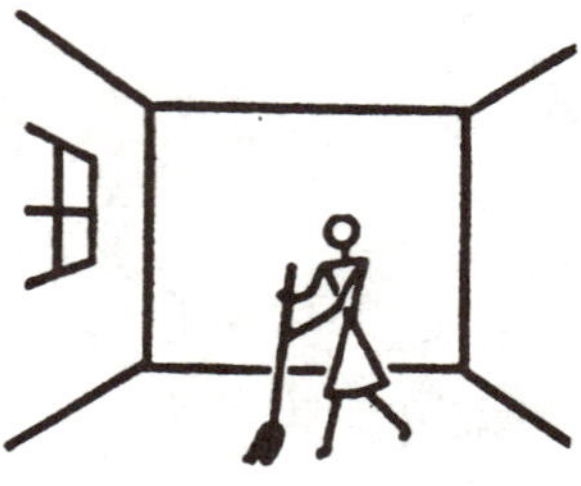

It is her house.
She is a housewife.

housewife [ˈhaus-waif]

Put your fingers across one another like this.

I have my first and second fingers across one another.

Across?
These two lines go across one another.

My second finger is over and across my first finger.

Did you put your fingers across one another?
That is right.
You have your fingers across one another.

Now take a pencil and give a touch to one finger, and then a touch to the other and then put the pencil between them.
Do this with your eyes shut.

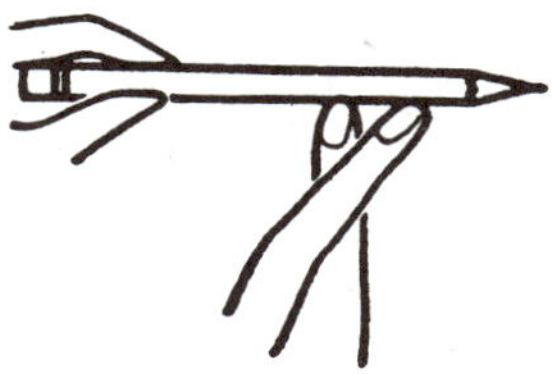

---

fingernails [ˈfiŋgəneilz]

touch [tʌtʃ]

You will have a strange feeling. Are two pencils touching your fingers, or is only one pencil touching them?

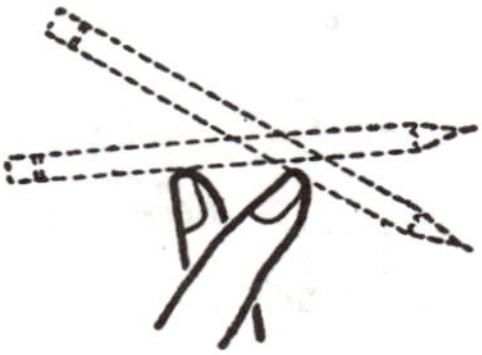

Do you have the strange feeling that two pencils are there? When you are touching one finger only, you seem to be touching the other?

Why is that? Here is the answer.

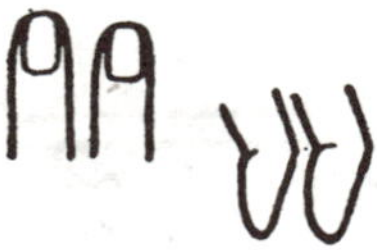

When the fingers are like this, or like this, they do their work together.

But when they are across one another they do not do their work together.
Then a touch to one sometimes seems to be a touch to the other.

feeling [ˈfi:liŋ]

touching [ˈtʌtʃiŋ]

What is their work?
What do the ends of our fingers do?
Their chief work is touching.

Those fingers are touching the cover of a book.
Touching gives us knowledge.
When our eyes are shut,

or when we are looking in another direction,
(she is touching the book)

or when we are not able to see,
we get knowledge through touching and feeling with our fingers.

chief [tʃi:f]

knowledge [ˈnɔlidʒ]
able [ˈeibl]

The chief work of the ends of our fingers is touching.
Here is a man who is not able to see.

That is a Braille book which he has before him.
He is reading the book with the ends of his fingers.

Braille letters and words are like this.
He is touching them with the ends of his fingers.

This other man is reading with his eyes.
He is not reading with his fingers.

What are those things on his nose?
They are his glasses.

Braille [breil]

What is the work of the eyes?

Seeing. Their work is seeing.

What is the work of the ears?

Hearing. Their work is hearing.

What is the work of the legs?

Walking. Walking is their chief work.

What is the work of the mouth?

Is talking or taking in food the chief work of the mouth?

What is the work of the hands? Taking things up, putting them down, getting things, giving things, making things.
We do things with our hands.

hearing ['hiəriŋ]

talking ['tɔ:kiŋ]
talk [tɔ:k]

a Is there more water in the sea than in a river?

b Give the names of three great discoveries.

c What is wool? What is cotton? Where do we get silk from?

d Why are thick clothes warmer than thin clothes?

e What is the chief work of the eyes, the ears, the mouth, and the fingers?

f What sorts of transport go on wheels?

g Where does smoke come from? Where does steam come from?

h Where do we get wood from?

Answers are on page 240.

a

b

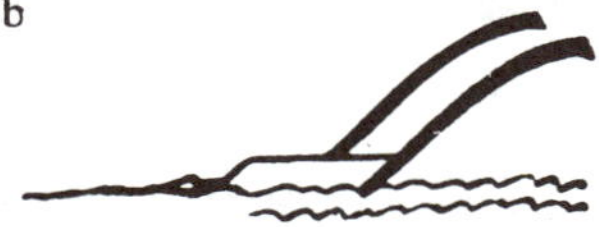

c

e

d

f

g

h

i

j

Answers are on page 240.

Answers to questions on pages 238-239.

Page 238

a There is more water in the sea than in a river.

b Fire, the wheel, and clothes were three great discoveries.

c Wool is the hair of sheep. Cotton is the hair round the seeds of the cotton plant. We get silk from the silkworm.

d Because thick clothes keep heat from going through it.

e The chief work of the eyes is seeing, of the ears is hearing, of the mouth is taking in food, and of the fingers is touching.

f Carts, cars, and trains go on wheels.

g Smoke comes from fire. Steam comes from boiling water.

h We get wood from trees.

Page 239

a a cart

b a plough

c a boot

d a looking-glass

e a skirt and a shirt

f a wheel

g a fire

h a spade

i a roll of cloth

j an umbrella

Seeing and hearing and touch are three of our senses.
We get knowledge through our eyes (seeing), through our ears (hearing), and through our fingers (touching).
These are three of our chief senses.

Another sense is taste.

This is a man's tongue.

These are his lips.
This is his chin.

The chief work of the tongue is tasting.

Here is some white powder on a plate.
It may be salt or it may be sugar.
Which is it— salt or sugar?

She is tasting the powder.
She has some of it on her finger.
She is putting some of the powder on her tongue. She is tasting it.

sense [sens]
tongue [tʌŋ]
lip [lip]

powder ['paudə*]
sugar ['ʃugə*]

We get salt from the sea.
The water in the sea has salt in it.

We get salt from salt mines.
Some mines are deep.
They go far down into the earth.

We get sugar from plants. We get it from the stems of some plants.

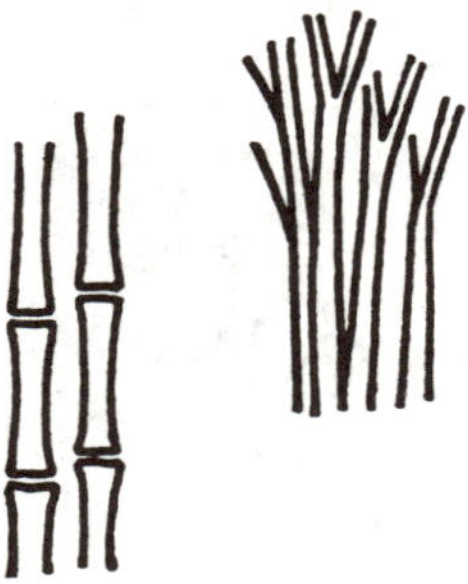

We get sugar from the roots of some plants.

The salt or sugar which we put in our food is a white powder.

mine [main]

deep [di:p]

The taste of sugar is sweet.

This is a cake.

It has white sugar on the top. Cakes with sugar on them are very sweet.

Salt has a salt taste.
Sugar has a sweet taste.
To the eye salt and sugar seem the same.

sweet [swi:t]
cake [keik]

This is an orange.

This is its peel.

Some oranges are sweet. But the taste of their peel is bitter.

But to the tongue they are very different.

Their taste is very different.

Salt

Sugar

top [tɔp]
bitter [ˈbitə*]

What is the work of the nose?
What do we do with our noses?
She has a flower in her hand.
She is smelling the flower.

Some flowers have a sweet smell.
Some flowers have no smell.

This is grass.
These flowers are in a garden.
They have a sweet smell.

These are pigs.
Some pigs arc dirty.
Some pigs are clean.
(See page 125.)
The smell of dirty pigs is not sweet.
It is a bad smell.

This is smoke.

This is a fire.

Some smoke has a good smell.
The smell may not be sweet, but it may be a good smell.
He is smoking a pipe.
Is the smell of the smoke good?

is smelling [iz'smeliŋ]
smell [smel]
grass [grɑ:s]

garden ['gɑ:dn]
is smoking [iz'smoukiŋ]

We see things with our eyes and we see their colours.
Here are some names of colours:

green	red
blue	yellow
white	gray

The sky is blue.

It is blue when it is clear.
The colour of some clouds is white.
Other clouds are gray.

What is the colour of grass and leaves in spring?
Grass and leaves in spring are green.
What is the colour of this girl's lips?
Her lips are red.

The sun is yellow.

Sometimes when it is going down

or coming up
it is red.

This flame
is yellow.

colour ['kʌlə*]
green [gri:n]
blue [blu:]

red [red]
yellow ['jelou]
gray [grei]

We see things with our eyes. We see the sizes and colours of things.
Sometimes things seem to our eyes greater or smaller than they are.
They are not what they seem.

This man is tall.

This man is short.

This is a tall woman.

This is a short woman.

Here are two men.
Do they seem the same size?

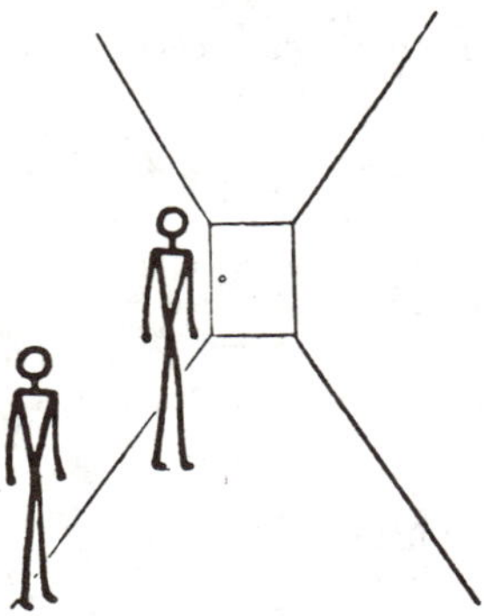

Which of them seems taller?
Does the man who is farther seem taller than the man who is nearer?
The pictures of them are the same size.
The lines in the picture make the man who is nearer seem shorter.

tall [tɔ:l]

taller [tɔ:lə*]
shorter [ʃɔ:tə*]

Seeing, hearing, touch, taste, and smell are "the five senses". But we have more than five senses. Which are some of the other senses?

Our sense of how warm or how cold things are is another.
Here is some cold water with ice in it.
It is very cold.

Here is some water in a kettle.
The water is boiling.
Steam is coming out of the kettle.

Here are three basins.
The basin on the right has very warm water in it. The basin on the left has cold water in it. The basin in the middle has water which is not cold and not warm in it.

kettle [ˈketl]

I put my hands in the basins at the sides.
One of my hands is in the cold water; the other is in the warm water.
I keep them there for a time.

Now I am putting them together into the middle basin where the water is not cold and not warm.

What is this?
This water seems warm to one hand and it seems cold to the other!
It is the same water.
But is seems cold and warm at the same time!

Why is this?
It is because one hand was in warm water and the other in cold water before I put them in this middle basin.

Another sense is our sense of motion.
Here is a chair which goes round and round.

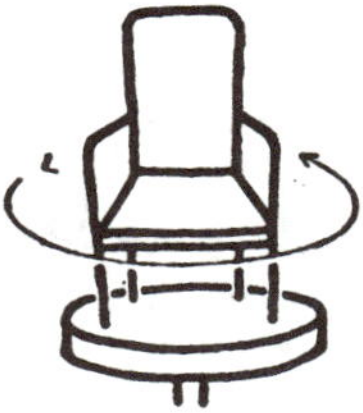

A man is on the chair.
He is going round and round...

At first he has a feeling that he is in motion.
He has the feeling that he is going round.
The chair, with the man on it, keeps on turning round at the same rate.
It does not go quicker.
It does not go slower.

After a time the man has a feeling that he is not in motion. But there is no change in the rate at which the chair is turning. It is going round the same number of times a minute.

rate [reit]

After a time, if the rate of turning is the same, the man seems to himself to be at rest (not in motion).

He is like all the men and women on the earth. We are all turning round all the time with the earth, but we seem to ourselves to be at rest.

We have no feeling that we are in motion.
This is because the rate of turning is the same.
The man is in motion.
He seems to himself to be at rest.

Here are three boys and a dog.
Two of the boys are taking a rest.
They are resting on their beds.
The other boy and the dog are in motion.

himself [him'self]

ourselves [auə'selvz]
are resting [ɑː'restiŋ]

Now, put a stop to the motion of the chair.
When you do that the chair is at rest. The man is not in motion.

But he has a feeling that he is turning round and round.
This is a picture of his feelings.

He is not turning round.
But he seems to himself to be turning round.
And everything round him seems to be turning round.
Why is this?

It is because change in our motion is the cause of our feelings of motion.
Through our sense of motion we get knowledge of changes in the rate and direction of our motion.

What is he doing?
He is hammering.

This is his hammer.

These are nails of
different sizes.

He is putting the lid on a box.
He is nailing down the lid of
the box.
The lid is on the top of the box.

The blows of the hammer make a
noise.
He is making a very loud noise.

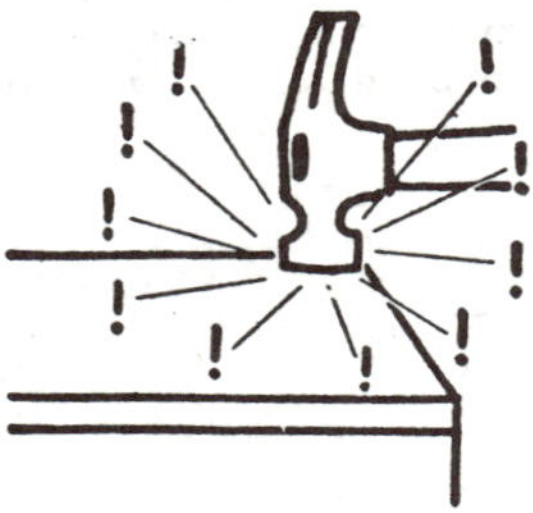

Mary has her hands over her
ears.
"What a noise!"
She is saying, "What a noise you
are making."

is hammering [iz'hæməriŋ]
is nailing [iz'neiliŋ]

noise [nɔiz]
loud [laud]

Some noises are loud.
These are guns.
Guns make loud noises.
Those guns make more noise than this gun.

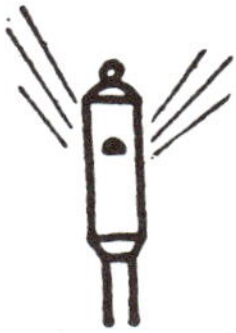

What is this?
It is a whistle.
It is a steam whistle. It is making a loud noise.

This boy has a pocket whistle. He is making some noise with it but not much noise.

This is music.

This is a song.

These are notes.

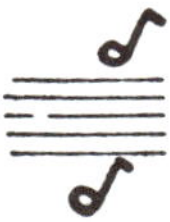

This is a high note.

This is a low note.

This is a very high mountain.

These are high mountains.

This is a high building.
It is a church.

This is a low building.

gun [gʌn]
whistle [ˈwisl]
music [ˈmju:zik]

song [sɔŋ]
note [nout]
church [tʃə:tʃ]

Noises and songs are sounds.
What are sounds?
They are the effects of waves in the air.

These
are waves in the sea.

These are waves in a cord. One end of the cord is fixed to a tree and the boy has the other end. He is shaking it up and down.

With every shake he sends a wave down the cord to the tree.

As the wave goes down the cord this part, which was up,

goes down. And this part, which was down, goes up.

sound [saund]
wave [weiv]

fixed [fikst]
shake [ʃeik]

These are waves in the air. They come to our ears.
They have effects in our ears and brains. Those effects are sounds.

Here is a brain.
The part of the brain which does the most work in hearing has the word HEARING on it.

"The most"?
Some things have water in them.
This cup has some water in it.
This bucket has more water in it.
The sea has the most water in it.

Some animals have brains: a horse has some brains; a monkey has more brains; and a man has the most brains of the three.

brain [brein]
the most [ðə'moust]

bucket ['bʌkit]
monkey ['mʌŋki]

I have two dollars.
You have twenty dollars.
He has a thousand dollars.
He has more money than we have.
You have more than I have.
He has the most money.

I have less money than he has.
I have less than you have.
I have the least money.

The most	$ 1000	
More	$ 20	Less
	$ 2	The least

This is the highest note.

This is a lower note,

but it is higher than this note.

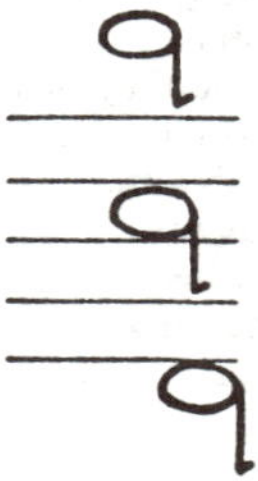

Which is the lowest note of the three?

Farming is an important sort of work.

Is it more important than banking?

the least [ðə'li:st]
the highest [ðə'haiist]
lower [louə*]

higher ['haiə*]
the lowest [ðə'louist]

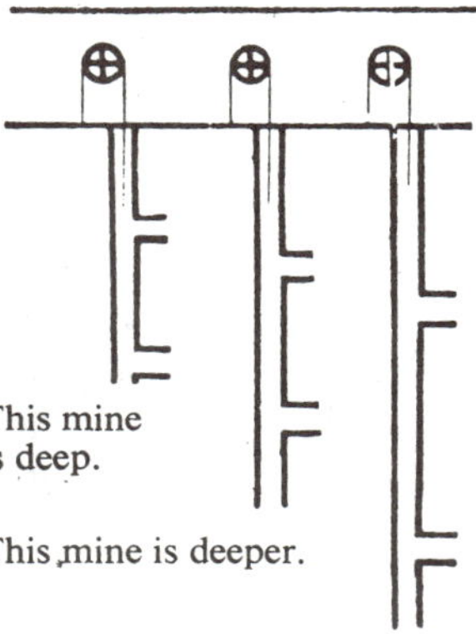

This mine is deep.

This mine is deeper.

This mine is the deepest of the three.

This is a good book.

These are two other good books.

One of them is better than the others.
It is the best book of the three.

This plate has some salt on it.

This plate has more salt on it.

This plate has the most salt on it.

It has more salt on it than the other plates.

This is a bad fire.

This is a worse fire.

This is the worst fire of the three.

deeper [di:pə*]
the deepest [ðə'di:pist]

the best [ðə 'best]
the worst [ðə 'wə:st]

She is looking at herself in a looking-glass.
Again and again, every day, she takes a look at herself in a glass.

Whenever she sees a looking-glass she goes to it and takes a look at herself.

Why?

Because looking at herself in the glass gives her pleasure.
She is beautiful. She sees that she is beautiful.

Looking at himself in the glass gives him no pleasure.
It gives him pain. Why?
He sees himself. Is he beautiful?

whenever [wen'evə*]
pleasure ['pleʒə*]

beautiful ['bju:təf*u*l]
pain [pein]

"Pleasure"? What is that?
"Pain"? What is that?

Put your finger in the flame.
No, I will not. Why not?
Because of the pain.

Here is a nail. You put your fingernail over this nail, and I will give it a blow with this hammer.

No, you will not. I see what pain is now. I see what the sense of the word "pain" is now.
This is another use of the word "sense".

That is pain. Pleasure is the opposite of pain.
"Opposite"? Good is the opposite of bad.

Good weather. The day is bright. The air is warm. The sky is blue. They are happy.

Bad weather. The wind is blowing. The rain is falling. It is cold. It is wet. They are unhappy.

Bright is the opposite of dark.

White is the opposite of black.

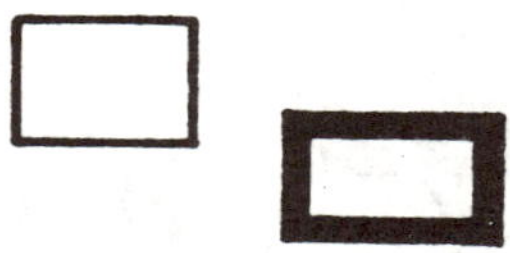

Warm is the opposite of cold.

What is the opposite of dry?
(See page 128.)
What is the opposite of happy?

unhappy [ʌnˈhæpi]

Which of these is a high building? What is the other?

What is the opposite of narrow? Is this street narrow?

Up is the

opposite of down.

In is the opposite of out.

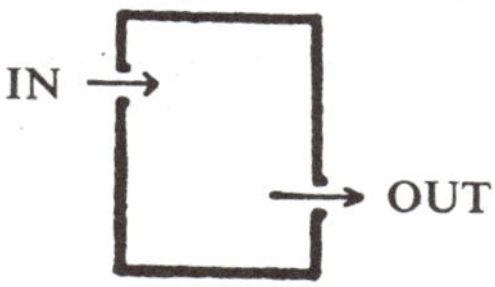

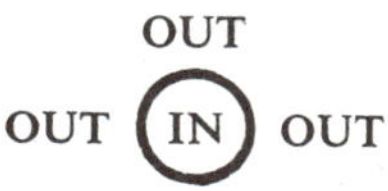

To is the opposite of from.

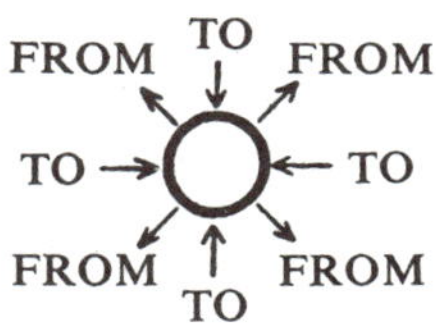

Pleasure is the opposite of pain.

Beautiful things give us pleasure.

When she sees herself in the glass,
she sees that she is beautiful.
That gives her pleasure.

When I say that she is beautiful,
that gives her pleasure.

There is a smile on her face now.

Why is the smile there?

It is there because she has a feeling of pleasure.
Her pleasure is the cause of her smile.
She is saying to herself,
"I am beautiful."

She is saying to herself that she is beautiful.

A smile does not make a sound.
A laugh makes a sound.

A laugh is a smile with a sound.

---

smile [smail]

laugh [la:f]

This is a great painting by Leonardo.

Its name is the Mona Lisa.

The picture is beautiful. That is certain.

Was the woman beautiful? Was Lisa herself beautiful? That is not certain.

I have my idea of that.

He has his idea.

She had her idea. We may have different ideas of how beautiful that woman was.

There is no measure of the beautiful.

---

painting [peintiŋ]

certain [ˈsə:tn]

She may or may not be beautiful.
But it is certain that she has a smile on her lips.
That is certain.

It is not certain that she is beautiful.

---

2 + 2 = 4. Two and two are equal to four. That is certain.

2 + 2 = 5. Two and two are not equal to five.
That is certain.

It is certain that 2 + 2 = 4.

---

a is equal to *b*, and *b* is equal to *c*, and *c* is equal to *d*.
So *a* is equal to *d*.
Things which are equal to the same things are equal to one another.

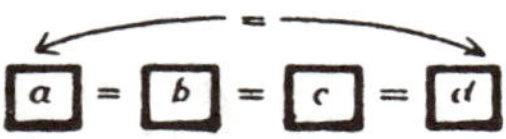

Things which are like one another may be equal or they may not.

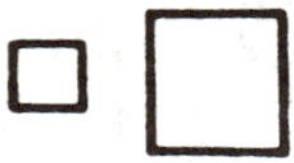

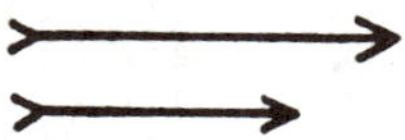

These two are like one another but they are not equal.

A smile is like a laugh.
But a laugh makes a sound.

This girl is laughing. She is happy.

She has a fall. She gives a cry.
Now she is crying.
She is not laughing now.
She is crying. Why?

Because she gave her knee a blow in her fall.

This is her knee. →

She was on her feet.

Then she was on her face. She had a fall.

The fall was the cause of the blow to her knee

The blow was the cause of the pain in her knee.

And the pain in her knee was the cause of her crying.

---

is laughing [iz'lɑ:fiŋ]

cry [krai]
is crying [iz'kraiiŋ]

Pleasure and pain are feelings. We have feelings of pleasure and pain.
Here are some pleasures.

He is on the sand at the seaside, looking at and hearing the sound of the waves and warming himself in the sun.
These are pleasures.

Now he is taking a swim in the sea.

He is swimming through the waves. He is a good swimmer. To a good swimmer, swimming is a pleasure.

Now he is resting in the sun again after his swim.

After the water the sun on his skin is a pleasure to him.

sand [sænd]
seaside ['si:'said]
warming ['wɔ:miŋ]
swim [swim]

swimmer ['swimə*]
swimming ['swimiŋ]
skin [skin]

Pleasure and pain are feelings.

When we put our fingers on things we have feelings—feelings of touch or of heat and cold. But this is another use of the word "feeling".

The man is feeling the bit of wood with his fingers.
Is it rough or is it smooth?

This is rough.

This is smooth.

Things which give us pleasure have an attraction for us.
But it is not the same sort of attraction as the attraction between the earth and the moon.
(See pages 202-203.)

Our feeling of this attraction is named "desire".
When we have pleasure we have a desire for the pleasure to go on and go on...
Time goes on. The hands of the clock go on. Our feelings may or may not go on.

rough [rʌf]

smooth [smu:ð]
desire [di'zaiə*]

Some desires are stronger than others.
This baby sees the cat and he sees his ball.

The cat has an attraction for him.
He has a desire for the cat.

His ball has an attraction for him.
He has a desire for the ball.

Which will he go to?
If his desire for the cat is stronger than his desire for the ball, he will go to the cat.

He went to the cat.
His desire for the cat was stronger.

All our desires are for things which seem good to us. They may not be good. Our ideas of them may be wrong.

---

cat [kæt]

wrong [rɔŋ]

We get knowledge by putting questions.
That is one way of getting knowledge.
The answers may give us knowledge or they may not.

When the answers are right, they give us knowledge.
When they are wrong they do not give us knowledge.
2 + 2 = 4 Right
2 + 2 = 5 Wrong

How far is the sun from the earth?
Which is the right answer:
"It is two miles away"
or "It is much more than two miles away"?
Which is the wrong answer to the question?

Which is his right hand?

Which is his left hand?
He is facing you.

Now he has his back to you.

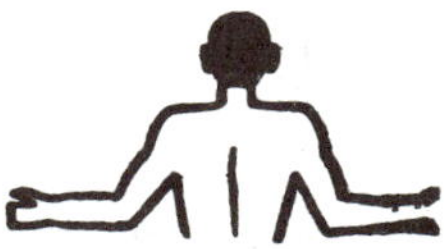

Which is his left hand now, and which is his right?

way [wei]

away [ə'wei]
is facing [iz'feisiŋ]

Our senses—seeing, hearing, touching, tasting, and smelling—are ways through which we get knowledge.
Our ideas come to us through our senses.

This is a doorway.

The way into the room is through the door.
The way out of the room is through the door.

"Which is the way to the station?"
"Take the first street to the right."

This man had no knowledge of the way to the station.
Now he has the knowledge.

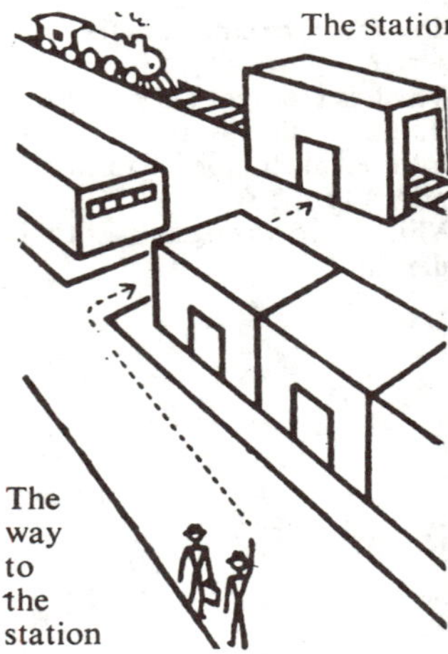

doorway [ˈdɔ:wei]

We get knowledge in different ways—through our senses,

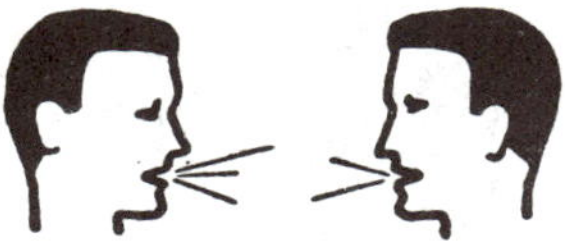

through talk with other men,

through the work we do with our hands and our heads, and through books.

These are all ways of getting knowledge.

Knowledge is very important. It is important in itself. And it is important as a way to other things. A man who has no knowledge is of no use to other men.

Is the word "use" part of your knowledge of English?
(See page 219.)
Knowledge gives us light. It makes things clearer to us.

clearer ['kliərə*]

This is a boy.

He will be a man.

He was a baby.

He seems to be about twelve years old now.

He gets up every morning at seven.

He gets out of bed and gives himself a good wash.

Every night he has a long sleep in his bed.

He goes to bed at eight every night.

He puts his clothes on.

He says "Good morning" to his mother and father and takes his place at the table.

sleep [sli:p]

At school he sees his friends and does his work.

He keeps his thoughts on his work.

He does not let his thoughts go off to other things.

At play after school he sends the ball a long way.

He makes it go a long way.

Then he comes back from school.

Here he is with the family again.

thought [θɔ:t]

play [plei]

Men are persons. They have their work.

They put and take things

 and give

 and get them.

They come and go.

→

They see and

say things,

keep things,

and let them (go),

make and

send them.

Some seem happier than others.
All these sorts of things are done by men and women.
Things are put and taken by them.
Things are given and got by them.
Things are seen and said by them.
Things are kept and let go by them.
Things are made and sent by them

done [dʌn]
taken [ˈteikən]

given [ˈgivn]
seen [siːn]

Eve saw the apple.

She took it.

She gave it to Adam.
Eve did these things.

The apple was seen by her.
It was taken by her.
It was given by her to Adam.
These things were done by Eve.

We may say this in two ways.
She saw the apple and took it and gave it to Adam.

This may be said in two ways.
The apple was seen by Eve, and taken and given by her to Adam.

Eve [i:v]

Adam ['ædəm]

I will do it.
I am doing it.
I did it.
They will see it.
They are taking it.
They gave it.
DO TAKE
SEE GIVE

It will be done by me.
It is being done by me.
It was done by me.
It will be seen by them.
It is being taken by them.
It was given by them.
DONE TAKEN
SEEN GIVEN

I will say it.
I said it.
I made it.
I kept it.
I let it go.
I put it there.
I got it.
I sent it.
SAY MAKE KEEP
LET PUT
GET SEND

It will be said by me.
It was said by me.
It was made by me.
It was kept by me.
It was let go by me.
It was put there by me.
It was got by me.
It was sent by me.
SAID MADE KEPT
LET PUT
GOT SENT

Every statement or question in this book has one or more of these sixteen words in it:

be	come	give	make
have	go	get	send
do	put	keep	see
seem	take	let	say

The first of these words, BE, comes into more statements than any other. Here it is. It goes like this:

	Past	*Present*	*Future*
I	was	am	will be
He She It	was	is	will be
We You They	were	are	will be

Here are the other fifteen words. They go like this:

	Past	Present	Future
	had	have	will have
	did	do	will do
I	seemed	seem	will seem
	came	come	will come
	went	go	will go
We	put	put	will put
	took	take	will take
	gave	give	will give
	got	get	will get
You	kept	keep	will keep
	let	let	will let
	made	make	will make
They	sent	send	will send
	saw	see	will see
	said	say	will say

	Past	*Present*	*Future*
	had	has	will have
	did	does	will do
	seemed	seems	will seem
	came	comes	will come
He	went	goes	will go
	put	puts	will put
	took	takes	will take
She	gave	gives	will give
	got	gets	will get
	kept	keeps	will keep
It	let	lets	will let
	made	makes	will make
	sent	sends	will send
	saw	sees	will see
	said	says	will say

In English we do not make statements like this:

She gave you money to I. That is wrong.

We make statements like this:

She gave your money to me. That is right.

I	my	me	we	our	us
you	your	you	you	your	you
he	his	him			
she	her	her	they	their	them
it	its	it			

In English we make COMPARISONS like this:

good	better	best
bad	worse	worst
much	more	most
little	less	least
beautiful	more beautiful	most beautiful
small	smaller	smallest
bright	brighter	brightest
short	shorter	shortest
thin	thinner	thinnest

In English we make changes in names like this:

1 cat (dog, boot, day, nose, face...)	2 or more cats (dogs, boots, days, noses, faces...)
1 glass (watch, brush...)	2 glasses (watches, brushes...)
1 body (cry, baby...)	2 bodies (cries, babies...)
1 knife (leaf, shelf...)	2 knives (leaves, shelves...)
1 tooth, foot	2 teeth, feet
1 man, woman	2 men, women

1 or more sheep, scissors, trousers

Wörterverzeichnis

Anmerkungen:

1. **Kursivbuchstaben,** die in der Lautschrift vorkommen, müssen nicht unbedingt gesprochen werden.
2. **Die ing-Form**

   schildert den Verlauf einer nicht abgeschlossenen Handlung, sie wird gebildet durch:

   Grundform des Zeitworts + ing.

   I am reading (now) = ich lese (gerade).
   We are reading (now) = wir lesen (gerade).
3. **Im Wörterverzeichnis verwendete Abkürzungen**

(*pl.*) = Mehrzahl (Plural)
(*sg.*) = Einzahl (Singular)

A

a [ə] ein (e, -er) 8
able ['eibl] fähig 235
about [ə'baut] ungefähr 186
account [ə'kaunt] Rechnung 230
across [ə'krɔs] von einer Seite zur anderen 219
Adam ['ædəm] Adam 275
addition [ə'diʃən] Zusammenzählen, Addition 229
aeroplane ['ɛərəplein] Flugzeug 95
after ['ɑːftə*] hinter 30
again [ə'gen] wieder 39
air [ɛə*] Luft 95
all [ɔːl] alle 49
am [æm] bin 4
America [ə'merikə] Amerika 136
amount [ə'maunt] Menge, Betrag 217
an [ən] ein (e, -er) 25
and [ənd] und 23
angle ['æŋgl] Winkel 155
animal ['æniməl] Tier 91
another [ə'nʌðə*] ein andere(r, -s) 61
answer ['ɑːnsə*] Antwort 30
apple ['æpl] Apfel 82
April ['eiprəl] April 175
are [ɑː*] sind 5
arm [ɑːm] Arm 25
as ... as ... [əz ... əz] so ... wie 182
at [æt; ət] an 29
attempt [ə'tempt] Versuch 159
attraction [ə'trækʃən] Anziehungskraft 200
August ['ɔːgəst] August 175
autumn ['ɔːtəm] Herbst 176
away [ə'wei] entfernt 269

B

baby ['beibi] Baby, Säugling 49
back [bæk] Rückseite 84
bad [bæd] schlecht 98
bag [bæg] (Reise)Tasche 122

C

D

E

F

I

J

K

L

M

N

Q

R

S

something [ˈsʌmθiŋ] etwas 150
sometimes [ˈsʌmtaimz] manchmal 188
son [sʌn] Sohn 108
song [sɔŋ] Lied 253
sort [soːt] Art 106
sound [saund] Geräusch 254
south [sauθ] Süden 144
spade [speid] Spaten 228
spoon [spuːn] Löffel 77
spring [spriŋ] Frühling 176
square [skwɛə*] Quadrat 202
stamp [stæmp] Briefmarke 136
star [stɑː*] Stern 144
state [steit] Staat 136
statement [ˈsteitment] Feststellung 207
station [ˈsteiʃən] Bahnhof 132
steam [stiːm] Dampf 93
stem [stem] Stengel 92
step [step] Stufe 137
stick [stik] Stock 180
stocking [ˈstɔkiŋ] Strumpf 81
story [ˈstɔːri] Geschichte 139
straight [streit] gerade 159
street [striːt] Straße 28
strong [strɔŋ] fest 161
stronger [ˈstrɔŋgə*] fester 162
sugar [ˈʃugə] Zucker 241
summer [ˈsʌmə] Sommer 176
sun [sʌn] Sonne 142
Sunday [ˈsʌndi] Sonntag 134
support [səˈpɔːt] Stütze 163
sweet [swiːt] süß 243
swim [swim] Bad 266
swimmer [ˈswimə*] Schwimmer 266
swimming [ˈswimiŋ] Schwimmen 266

T

table [ˈteibl] Tisch 10
tail [teil] Schwanz 49
take [teik] nehme(n) 14; 278-9
taken [ˈteikən] genommen 274
(is) taking [(iz) ˈteikiŋ] nimmt (gerade) 14
talk [tɔːk] sprechen 237
talking [ˈtɔːkiŋ] Sprechen 237
tall [tɔːl] groß 246
taller [ˈtɔːlə*] größer 246
taste [teist] Geschmack 105
(is) tasting [(iz) ˈteistiŋ] versucht (gerade) 105
taxi [ˈtæksi] Taxi 132
teacher [ˈtiːtʃə*] Lehrer 138
(is) teaching [(iz) ˈtiːtʃiŋ] bringt (gerade) bei 138
teeth [tiːθ] (*pl.*) Zähne (*pl.*) 103
ten [ten] zehn 36
than [ðæn] als 177
that [ðæt] jene(r, -s) 8
the [ðə] (vor Mitlauten) der, die, das, die (*pl.*) 10
the [ði] (vor Selbstlauten) der, die, das, die (*pl.*) 95
their (*pl.*) [ðɛə*] ihre (*pl.*) 78
them (*pl.*) [ðem] sie; ihnen (*pl.*) 47
then [ðen] dann 47
there [ðɛə*] dort 4
these (*pl.*) [ðiːz] dies(e) (*pl.*) 10
they (*pl.*) [ðei] sie (*pl.*) 2
thick [θik] dick 98
(the) thickest [(ðə) ˈθikist] (der, die, das) dickste 181
thin [θin] dünn 98
thing [θiŋ] Gegenstand 37
thirteen [ˈθəːˈtiːn] dreizehn 145
thirty [ˈθəːti] dreißig 100

U

W

V—X

Y—Z

Die Sprachentitel in unserer Reihe:

humboldt-taschenbücher (in Klammern die Bandnummer)

praktischer ratgeber

Kinderspiele (47)
Erziehen (80)
Kinder basteln (172)
Leichter lernen (191)
Kinder raten (193)
Schönheitstips (203)
Erste Hilfe (207)
Vornamen (210)
Buchführung (211)
Katzen (212)
Haushaltstips (213)
Ruhestand (216)
Dackel (224)
Traumbuch (226)
Geschäftsbriefe (229)
Kneippkur (230)
Partybuch (231)
Unser Baby (233)
Anstreichen (234)
Werken mit Holz (235)
Zuckerkranke (236)
Schulsorgen? (239)
Nähen (240)
Reden f. jed. Anlaß (247)
Herzinfarkt (250)
So bewirbt man sich (255)
Speisepilz/Giftpilz (256)
Pudel (258)
Komma-Lexikon (259)
Schulanfang (262)
Kinder schenken (264)
Zimmerpflanzen (270)
Kakteen (271)
Handschriften (274)
Angst erkennen (276)
Wellensittiche (285)
Gästebuch (287)
Weine (288)
Goldhamster (289)
Geschenke (290)
Taschenrechner (292)
Schäferhunde (298)
So schreibt man Briefe (301)
~ Liebesbriefe (377)
Gutes Benehmen (303)
Fotolexikon (308)
Verdauung (310)
Herz- u. Kreislauf (311)
Partnerwahl/Partnerschaft (312)
Gedächtnis/Konzentration (313)
Wie helfe ich krank. Hund (319)
Perf. Heimwerkstatt (320)
Einrichten-Repar.-Renov. (321)
Krankenversicherung (322)
Hundelexikon (332)
Außenarbeiten u. Haus (334)
Holzarbeiten z. Hause (335)
Autogenes Training (336)
Rückenschmerzen (339)
Heilpflanzen (342)
Schönheitspflege (343)
Ikebana (353)
Guter Schlaf (354)
Heilmassage (355)
Kanarienvögel u.a. (356)
Versicherungen (357)
Deutsche Weine (361)
Rheuma (364)
Allergien (365)
100 schönst. Kakteen (370)
Wie erziehe ich meinen Hund? (371)
Autofahren heute (375)
Landleben f. Städter (376)
Umzug kein Probl. (387)
Hautkrankheiten (388)
Schwangerschaft und Geburt (392)
300 alkoholfr. Mixgetränke (396)
Sauna (406)
Heilfasten (407)
Kopfschmerzen (408)
Behörden (409)

kochen

Mixgetränke (218)
Tiefkühlkost (219)
Schnellküche (220)
Kalte Küche (221)
Fleischgerichte (222)
Fischgerichte (223)
Grillen (245)
Schnellkochtopf (251)
Diät Zuckerkranke (257)
Diät Leber Galle (260)
Backen (269)
Mittelmeerküche (275)
Salate (286)
Fondues (294)
Preiswert kochen (295)
Leichte Kost (306)
Allerlei Suppen (307)
Schlankheitsküche (316)
Nachspeisen (317)
Italienische Küche (328)
Hackfleischgerichte (329)
Küchenbegriffe (340)
Kräuter, Gewürze (341)
Käselexikon (358)
Jugoslaw. Küche (359)
Chines. Küche (366)
Tontopfgerichte (367)
Früchte zubereiten (378)
Geflügelgerichte (379)
Geschenke a. d. eigenen Küche (404)
Französ. Küche (405)

freizeit – hobby – quiz

Frag 3300 × (23)
Briefmarkensammler (58)
Wer weiß es? (68)
Frag mich was! (79)
Frag noch was! (83)
Schach (85)
Frag weiter! (90)
Kreuzworträtsellex. (91)
Wer ist das? (118)
Wer knobelt mit? (143)
Zaubertricks (164)
Zierfische (171)
Quiz i. Wort u. Bild (174)
Spielen Sie mit! (190)
Spaß m. Tests (195)
Kartenspiele (199)
Der Garten (202)
Fotografieren (204)
Intelligenztest (225)
Filmen (232)
Mit Zahlen spielen (237)
Skat (248)
Mikroskopieren (249)
Gartenarbeit (252)
Garten – angelegt (254)
Rätsel, leicht gelöst (263)
Modelleisenbahn (266)
Basteln mit Stoff (267)
Zeichnen (268)
Mein Aquarium (272)
Bridge (273)
Bergwandern (278)
Steine sammeln (280)
Gesellschaftsspiele (281)
Brettspiele (282)
Patiencen (293)
Schach ohne Partner (299)
Glücksspiele (309)
Häkeln (314)
Stricken (315)
Pfeife rauchen (318)
Taschenb. d. Jagd (325)
Filmen-Techn.-Motive (330)
Am Brunnen v. d. Tore 100 Volks- u. Wanderlieder (331)
Fotomotive (346)
Rosen (347)
Balkon, Terrasse, Dachgarten (350)
Schreibspiele u.a. (352)
Tanzen (362)
Schachtaktik (363)
Bauernmalerei (368)
Batik (369)
Malen (381)
Modellflug (383)
Töpfern (384)
Trockenblumen (385)
Schach Eröffnungsspiele (386)
Fotolabor (389)
Gitarrenschule (390)
Stoffmalerei (394)
Campingurlaub (399)
Volkslieder (400)
200 Spiele (401)
Glasmalerei (402)
Obst+Gemüse (403)

sport für alle

Yoga (82)
Segelsport (123)
Selbstverteidigung (178)
Reitlehre (205)
Angeln/Fischen (206)
Gymnastik (228)
Skilanglauf (241)
Skisport-Berater (242)
Kegeln (243)
Tennis (253)
Ski – aktuell (265)
Tauchen (277)
Golf (279)
Sportschießen (300)
Taschenb. d. Sports (302)
Taschenlex. Wassersport (304)
Windsurfing Wasserski (305)
Pferde u. Reiten (323)
Sportbegriffe v. A-Z 324)
Kanu (326)
Meeresangeln (327)
Yoga+Gymnastik (333)
Pferderennen/Wetten (348)
Lex. d. Segelsports (349)
Squash (360)
Judo – Karate (372)
Tennis-Training (374)
Welches Pferd? (380)
Lauf dich fit (382)
Judo f. Jugendl. (391)
Ponys (393)
Tennis-Gymnastik (395)
Segelsurfen (398)

sprachen

Englisch I (11)
Französisch I (40)
Italienisch I (55)
Spanisch I (57)
Englisch II (61)
Russisch (81)
Italienisch II (108)
Französisch II (109)
Dänisch (124)
Serbokroatisch (183)
Englisch lernen (Bild) (296)
Französisch lernen (Bild) (297)
Italienisch (Bild) (344)
Spanisch lernen (Bild) (345)
Griechisch f. Urlaub (373)

moderne information

Wirtschaftslexikon (24)
Wörterb. Philosophie (43)
Musikinstrumente (70)
Rausch d. Drogen (140)
Mengenlehre (142)
Computerrechnen (146)
Transistoren (151)
Betriebswirtschaft (153)
Elektrotechnik (163)
Psychoanalyse (168)
Wortschatz (170)
Taschenlex. Antike (180)
Die neuesten Wörter (187)
Datenverarbeitung (200)
Pflanzen bestimmen (208)
Tiere bestimmen (209)
Weltatlas (227)
Psychologie (238)
PSI (244)
Volkswirtschaft (246)
Management-Begriffe (261)
Erkenne dich/andere (283)
Astrologie (284)
Weltgeschichte (291)
Wörterb. Psychologie (337)
Mikroprozessoren (338)
Baustile (351)
Malerei – sehen u. verst. (397)